Klaus Theo Brenner
Villen und Landhäuser
Architektonische Entwürfe
Villas and Country Houses
Architectonic Designs

KLAUS THEO BRENNER

VILLEN UND LANDHÄUSER

VILLAS AND COUNTRY HOUSES

jovis

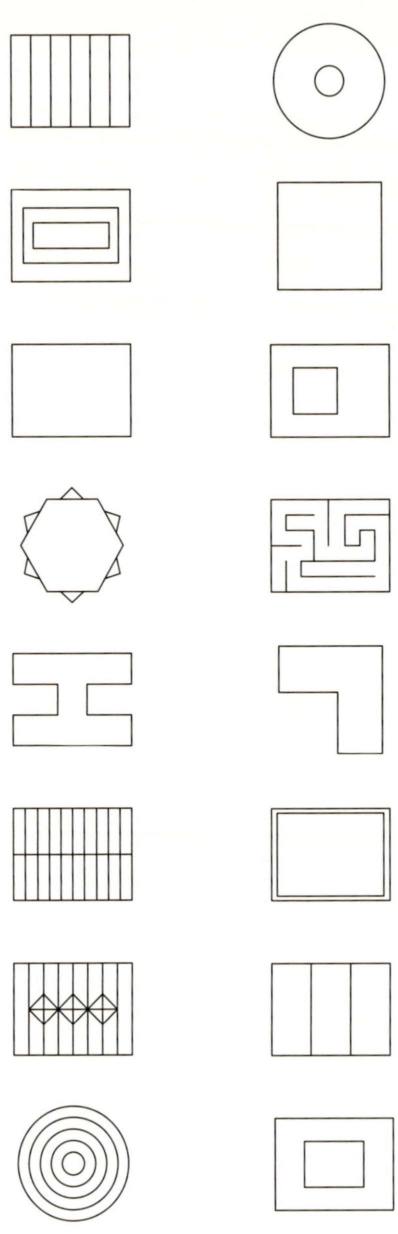

Treppenhaus   Rundling

Zikkurat   Würfel

Schwebendes Haus   Turm

Schraube   Labyrinth

Hofhaus   Winkel

Glashaus   Bastion

Forsthaus   Terrassenhaus

Kuppel   Atriumhaus

Foreword

The projects gathered here are designs for villas and country-houses; designs for a specific architectural task – the building of large houses that make exacting demands on space, individuality and architectonic quality. The villa is an enduring theme, on the basis of which clients and architects have always been able to demonstrate their capacities, skill and – not least – good taste. The history of the villa is still being written, even though this type of classical architectural task (like many others) has become quite rare; as rare as good taste, which represents a fundamental criterion of quality, no matter what style we are building in, but is difficult to pin down – not only, but perhaps especially in the construction of villas.

While the villa is perhaps not the most important, but still a relevant theme with considerable entertainment value, therefore, the question of its architecture is repeatedly raised: as the concern of architects, but also of potential clients. The designs shown here represent a number of suggestions, which – in form and character – differ fundamentally from other suggestions put forward by contemporary architectural debate. At the same time, however, they reveal affinities with older and more recent examples of architectural history. All the designs in this series have a strong **individual character**, which strikes us immediately. And yet they all share an aesthetic quality that could be described as narrative; vividly expressive and very much present as architectonic objects, but relatively simple in formal structure. In each case, the overall form determines the structure down to its details. It is, so to speak, an architectonic catalogue of themes to choose from freely, but each of the designs requires adaptation to the concrete requirements of the building client in its realisation. The aim of this spectrum of ideas is to stimulate the imagination, but it by no means exhausts the list of conceivable solutions. Architecture is shown, which – despite its great individuality and diversity of form – does not deny the cubic origins of architecture, the fact that **»miracles come from the box«**. Thus all the designs together – from the cube to the screw – represent a family of »specific objects« (Donald Judd) and a contribution to the issue of type and form in the field of the contemporary villa.

Vorwort

Die hier versammelten Entwürfe zeigen Villen und Landhäuser; Entwürfe für eine besondere Bauaufgabe, große Häuser mit einem hohen Anspruch an Raum, Individualität und architektonische Qualität. Die Villa war immer ein Thema, anhand dessen Bauherren und Architekten ihre Kapazität, ihr Können und nicht zuletzt ihren guten Geschmack demonstrieren konnten. Die Geschichte der Villa wird fortgeschrieben, auch wenn dieser Typus (wie viele andere) als klassische Bauaufgabe eher rar geworden ist, ebenso rar wie der gute Geschmack, der, egal in welchem Stile wir bauen, ein zwar grundlegendes, aber nur schwer konkretisierbares Qualitätskriterium darstellt, auch und gerade im Villenbau.

Ist die Villa also vielleicht nicht das bedeutendste, aber doch ein aktuelles Thema mit hohem Unterhaltungswert, so stellt sich immer wieder neu die Frage nach ihrer Architektur: ein Anliegen von Architekten, aber auch von potentiellen Bauherren. Die hier gezeigten Entwürfe stellen ein Angebot dar, das sich in Form und Charakter von anderen Angeboten der zeitgenössischen Architekturdebatte grundlegend unterscheidet, aber gleichzeitig Verbindungslinien zu älteren und jüngeren Beispielen der Architekturgeschichte aufweist. Alle Entwürfe dieser Serie haben einen starken **individuellen Charakter**, der unmittelbar ins Auge springt. Und doch ist allen Entwürfen eine ästhetische Qualität gemeinsam, die man erzählerisch nennen könnte; stark im bildhaften Ausdruck und präsent als architektonisches Objekt, aber relativ einfach in der von der jeweiligen Gesamtform bestimmten formalen Struktur bis ins Detail. Ein architektonischer Themenkatalog zur freien Auswahl sozusagen, der im Falle der Realisierung den konkreten Bedürfnissen der Bauherren angepasst werden müsste. Mit diesem Ideenspektrum wollen wir die Phantasie anregen, die denkbaren Lösungen sind damit jedoch keinesfalls erschöpft. Es wird eine Architektur ausgebreitet, die bei aller Individualität und Formenvielfalt den kubischen Ursprung der Architektur, die Tatsache, dass **»die Wunder aus der Kiste kommen«** nicht verleugnet. So bilden alle Entwürfe zusammen, vom Würfel bis zur Schraube, eine Familie von »spezifischen Objekten« (Donald Judd) und einen Beitrag zur Frage nach Typus und Form der zeitgenössischen Villa.

Type

If one defines the city – like Max Weber – as a self-contained »settlement«, a »place« that does not consist of separate residential properties but of houses standing particularly close together, mostly wall to wall[1], one cannot attribute the villa – also known as the country-house due to its topographical situation – to urban architecture and must consequently regard it as a specific type. It ought therefore to be discussed according to different criteria from the urban row house with its diverse uses and, generally, several apartments above and beside one another[2]. The themes **urban row house** and **villa** with their categorical differences must be regarded as complementary. If the aesthetic criteria for the evaluation of urban architecture emerge essentially from the quality of its wall-like boundary to public space, whereby the façade has particular significance, the »villa«, by contrast, is open to discussion as an individual object and thus as an architectural volume with a three-dimensional effect. However, Max Weber also attributes the free-standing villa to capitalist money transactions and specifically to those who benefit from such money transactions and their resulting profits. As he maintains, those receiving the growing profits do not, as a rule, consume them in the urban location of their business headquarters, but outside this in their own house, some in suburbs of villas, some – indeed more – in rural »villeggiaturas«[3], which were distributed within a radius of more than 50 kilometres beyond the city borders of Berlin in the 19th/20th century, for example. This radius has grown even further now, so that today some people realise their desire for the villeggiatura on Mallorca. Even bearing in mind today's living conditions, let us start out from this categorical opposition between city house – country house or row house – villa (the term city villa is actually paradoxical, although it has become established). And let us take into account the fact that according to Max Weber, the villa has not only socialised itself in the form of »villa suburbs«, it has also moved closer to the city – but it can still be fundamentally distinguished in size, aura and individual space for realisation from the petit-bourgeois detached house (the »villette«) found amidst the monotonous settlements on the urban peripheries. Something of its size remains, but today we are concerned with a different type of villa to the classical villa that Rudolf Borchardt still regarded as ideal in his essay *Villa* dating from 1907. He viewed the villa colony of the German suburbs as an atrocity and believed that its inhabitants (whether moneyed or intellectual bourgeoisie) would – he remarks ironically – be horrified to see a »true« villa, for »what they finally set eyes on after a wearying path through white dust between oversized garden walls is a simplicity and bareness that people would be ashamed of in this country. None of the little towers, gables, bays and crenellations, by means of which the rented apartment dweller demonstrates his sense of sophistication when he is finally permitted to do as he pleases, no splendid facades in real or imitation stone, nor meaningful sayings above the doors, their old-world characters inviting us to enter Quisisana or Villa Amalie«.[4] The tourist from the German

Typus

Wenn man mit Max Weber Stadt als eine geschlossene »Siedelung«, eine »Ortschaft« bezeichnet, die nicht aus vereinzelten Behausungen besteht, sondern im Gegenteil aus Häusern, die besonders dicht, meist Wand an Wand stehen[1], kann man die Villa, die nach ihrer örtlichen Umgebung auch Landhaus genannt wird, nicht der städtischen Bebauung zurechnen und muss sie folgerichtig als einen Sondertypus betrachten, der nach anderen Kriterien diskutiert werden muss als das städtische Reihenhaus mit seinen vielfältigen Nutzungen und meist mehreren Wohnungen über- und nebeneinander[2]. Die Themen **städtisches Reihenhaus** und **Villa** sind in ihrer kategorischen Unterschiedlichkeit als komplementär zu betrachten. Ergeben sich die ästhetischen Kriterien der Bewertung von Stadtarchitektur im Wesentlichen aus der Qualität der wandartigen Begrenzung des öffentlichen Raums mit besonderer Bedeutung der Fassade, so steht die »Villa« als freistehendes Objekt und damit als dreidimensional wirkender, architektonischer Körper zur Diskussion. Allerdings ordnet Max Weber die freistehende Villa ebenfalls dem kapitalistischen Geldverkehr zu und dort speziell denen, die von diesem Geldverkehr und den daraus resultierenden Gewinnen profitieren. Wachsende Gewinne, wie er sagt, werden von den Bezugsberechtigten in der Regel nicht an dem großstädtischen Ort ihres geschäftlichen Sitzes konsumiert, sondern auswärts im eigenen Haus, teils in Villenvororten, teils aber noch mehr in ländlichen »Villeggiaturen«[3], die zum Beispiel im Berlin des 19./20. Jahrhunderts in einem Radius von gut 50 Kilometern über die Stadtgrenzen hinaus verteilt waren. Dieser Radius ist inzwischen größer geworden, sodass heutzutage manche Leute ihre Lust auf die Villeggiatura auf Mallorca ausleben. Gehen wir also von dieser kategorischen Gegensätzlichkeit Stadthaus – Landhaus oder Reihenhaus – Villa (der Begriff Stadtvilla ist, obwohl er sich eingebürgert hat, eigentlich paradox) auch unter den heutigen Lebensbedingungen aus und berücksichtigen wir dabei, dass die Villa nach Max Weber in Form von »Villenvororten« sich nicht nur vergesellschaftet hat, sondern auch an die Stadt herangerückt ist, sich aber in Größe, Aura und individuellem Entfaltungsspielraum grundsätzlich vom kleinbürgerlichen Einfamilienhäuschen (den »villette«) im Siedlungseinerlei der Stadtperipherien unterscheidet. Etwas ist übrig geblieben von ihrer Größe, allerdings haben wir es heute mit einem anderen Typus von Villa zu tun als dem klassischen, wie ihn Rudolf Borchardt in seinem Aufsatz *Villa* von 1907 noch als Ideal vorstellte. Ihm war die Villenkolonie der deutschen Vorstädte ein Gräuel und ihr Bewohner (Geld- oder Bildungsbürger) wäre, wie er ironisch anmerkt, beim Anblick einer »echten« Villa entsetzt, denn »was er nach dem ermüdenden Wege durch weißen Staub zwischen überhohen Gartenmauern endlich gewahr wird, ist eine Einfachheit und Kahlheit, deren man sich hierzulande schämen würde. Weder die Türmchen, Giebel, Erker und Zinnen, durch die der Mietshaus-Einwohner zeigt, welchen Sinn fürs Höhere er hat, wenn er einmal darf wie er will, weder Prunkfassaden aus echtem oder unechtem Stein, noch die sinnreichen Sprüche auf Spruchbändern über

villa suburb, if he travels to Italy, will »see little more than large, apparently quite spacious and comfortable houses, standing on rough grass and not in the best-kept condition, with working quarters and useful extensions, yellowing, with marks of mildew on the whitewash, the stone facades weather-beaten, the rendering cracked, moss on the paths and no flower beds or colour anywhere at all; lacking decoration, like German manor-houses. Is that the villa? It certainly is!«[5] Rudolf Borchardt, by the way, was in love with this classical type of Italian villa – the ideal image of which was Palladio's Villa Rotonda – to such an extent that he lived in a villa in the Lucca region himself for many years, working as a gardener. His chief concern was to establish a connection between a specific type of building's loss of social function and its decline into kitsch.

But let us take Villa Rotonda; doesn't this villa in particular – for everyone who has seen it – represent a classical high point, yet simultaneously mark the outset of a development celebrating the type of villa that is an **autonomous object**? Borchardt criticises this formal autonomy harshly, as well as the social ambitions associated with the architectonic ideal »villa«, to which it became stylised in the course of that development. Vehemently, he points out the economic realism, the »tool« character of the classical villa, the overthrow of which is certainly symbolised by the »Rotonda«, but was actually already laid out in the Roman Villa Hadriana. What stands out, however, becoming a defining factor in the modern concept of the villa, is its architectonic character as a toy, in combination with the utopia of landscape (however small the estate may be) as a counter-design to the city. And we will continue to concern ourselves with this toy for as long as there are clients and sites available.

If we now start out, therefore, from the assumption that today the villa as a luxurious building type, as a large residential house, even perhaps as a toy for the individual client, built as a free-standing structure in its own grounds, represents a special architectural task in Max Weber's sense – on a branch-line, as it were, leading away from other, perhaps more relevant tasks of urban architecture –, then the question of its architecture – generous and standing independently as a symbol – is as interesting as ever as a measure of the client's status and the architect's skill. The villa has become an autonomous work of art for the capitalist bourgeoisie. Around 1800, Schinkel was consistent inasmuch as he presented large and small palaces as well as urban houses or palatial homes among his collection of architectonic designs, but no villas, since this type of building was not relevant in Prussia until the growing bourgeoisie discovered and disseminated it in northern Europe. Seen in this way, the villa as an architectonic theme – admittedly, with severe restrictions by comparison to the classical, Italian type – has not only become an expressly

den Türen, die in Altfraktur zum Eintritt in Quisisana oder Villa Amalie einladen«.[4] Er, der Tourist aus dem deutschen Villenvorort wird, wenn er nach Italien reist, »überhaupt kaum etwas anderes sehen, als große, augenscheinlich recht geräumige und bequeme Wohnhäuser, im groben Rasen stehend und nicht zum besten gehalten, mit Ökonomiegebäuden und Nutzanbauten, recht gelb, Stockflecken auf der Tünche, die Steinfassaden verwitternd, der Bewurf rissig, Moos auf den Wegen und nirgend Teppichbeete und überhaupt Farbe, schmucklos nach Art deutscher Gutshöfe. Ist das die Villa? Es ist sie!«[5] Rudolf Borchardt war übrigens dermaßen vernarrt in diesen klassischen Typus der italienischen Villa, zu deren Idealbild Palladios Villa Rotonda geworden war, dass er selbst Jahre in einer Villa im Lucchesischen gelebt und als Gärtner gearbeitet hat. Worum es ihm im Wesentlichen ging, war, eine Beziehung herzustellen zwischen dem Verlust an sozialer Funktion eines Bautypus und dessen Verfall in Kitsch.

Aber die Villa Rotonda, stellt nicht gerade sie für jeden, der sie einmal gesehen hat, den klassischen Höhepunkt, gleichzeitig aber auch den Beginn einer Entwicklung dar, die den Typus der Villa als **autonomes Objekt** feiert? Diese formale Autonomie und die damit verbundenen gesellschaftlichen Ambitionen des architektonischen Ideals »Villa«, zu dem sie im Verlauf jener Entwicklung stilisiert wurde, kritisierte Borchardt hart, dabei vehement auf den ökonomischen Realismus, den Werkzeugcharakter der klassischen Villen verweisend, dessen Überwindung mit der »Rotonda« zwar symbolisiert wird, eigentlich aber in der römischen Villa Hadriana bereits angelegt war. Was nun jedoch hervortritt und für den modernen Begriff der Villa bestimmend wird, ist ihr architektonischer Spielzeugcharakter, verbunden mit einer Utopie von Landschaft (und sei das Grundstück noch so klein) als Gegenentwurf zur Stadt. Mit diesem Spielzeug werden wir uns beschäftigen, solange es Bauherren und Grundstücke dafür gibt.

Wenn wir nun davon ausgehen, dass die Villa als luxuriöser Bautyp, als großes Wohnhaus, ja vielleicht Spielzeug für den individuellen Bauherrn, auf eigenem Grundstück und freistehend im Garten gebaut, im Sinne Max Webers heute eine besondere Bauaufgabe, sozusagen im Nebengleis zu den anderen, vielleicht aktuelleren Aufgaben der Stadtarchitektur darstellt, ist die Frage nach ihrer Architektur – großzügig und unabhängig dastehend als Symbol – für den Status des Bauherrn ebenso wie für die Leistungsfähigkeit des Architekten nach wie vor interessant. Die Villa ist zum autonomen Kunstwerk für das kapitalistische Bürgertum geworden. Schinkel war um 1800 insofern konsequent, als er in seiner Sammlung architektonischer Entwürfe zwar große und kleine Schlösser zeigte und städtische Wohnhäuser oder Wohnpalais, aber keine Villen, da dieser Bautyp in Preußen kein Thema war, bevor das aufsteigende Bürgertum ihn als den seinen entdeckte und er sich im

bourgeois architectural task, but also, logically, a topic of Modernism. This has applied from its origins in the late 19th century up until the present day, with extremely different stylistic emphases: the strict Classicism of Peter Behrens in Germany; the picturesque tendency developed from the English country-house – elaborated by Muthesius and finding a unique interpretation in the work of Frank Lloyd Wright; the house as a machine, interpreted either stylistically in the sense of a space-ship, or as the so-called high-tech house (a type dating from early Modernism, which spread during the 60s and 70s); and not least – and from the point of view of influence the most important – the villa of classical Modernism resulting from the transformation of the classical type into the autonomous work of art. Both Mies van der Rohe and Le Corbusier represent this tendency. Colin Rowe: »In this we note a negation of volumes, a replacement by surfaces. These are designs that appear to be a perfect illustration of Giedion's principle of space-time, for which Bauhaus is so rightly famous. These are compositions that the eye is incapable of comprehending at a single glance.«[6] This contra-position pointed out by Colin Rowe – the classical-monumental type in the form of a symmetrically composed figure or architectonic group of rigid volumes as opposed to its defeat in Modernism –, has blocked or rather polarised architectural discussion unproductively for far too long. We attempt to demonstrate a way out of rigid Classicism and past the confusion of modernist compositions: the character of the house appears in a powerful physical form and unfolds as a three-dimensional, architectonic object, free-standing in its own garden.

Form

Transformation from a manor-house in the country to a bourgeois dwelling in the suburbs turned the villa into an architectonic toy for the well-to-do; initially, however, it continued to be tied to classical architectural language, sometimes more monumental, sometimes rather picturesque, often quite simply kitschy. Only with 20th century Modernism did it develop into an autonomous work of art. Both tendencies, if viewed in an antipodal way, are still very much alive and the ideological war between their propagandists continues unabated. There are architects and clients who maintain that a villa, due to its heroic history, can only be formed in a Classicist manner – and the Modernists claim precisely the opposite. The aim of the designs presented here is to evade this stylistic debate. We thematise the villa through the radical nature of its form as a concrete three-dimensional image, which addresses us directly and (or precisely because it) can be concretised in a conceptual way. The form implies a name for the house, or when looking at the house a name for it immediately occurs to the observer. So is this an architecture parlante? Not in the functionalist sense, as Kaufmann observed in the French architecture of the Revo-

nördlichen Europa ausbreiten konnte. So gesehen ist die Villa als architektonisches Thema mit zugegebenermaßen gravierenden Einschränkungen gegenüber dem klassisch-italienischen Typus nicht nur eine ausgesprochen bürgerliche Bauaufgabe, sondern konsequenterweise auch ein Thema der Moderne geworden, und zwar von ihren Ursprüngen im späten 19. Jahrhundert bis heute, mit extrem unterschiedlichen stilistischen Ausprägungen: der strenge Klassizismus zum Beispiel von Peter Behrens in Deutschland; die malerische Tendenz aus dem englischen Landhaus kommend, von Muthesius verarbeitet und in Frank Lloyd Wright eine ganz eigenständige Interpretation erfahrend; das Haus als Maschine, entweder stilistisch im Sinne eines Raumfahrzeugs oder als so genanntes High-Tech-Haus interpretiert (ein Typus aus der frühen Moderne, der sich in den 60er und 70er Jahren verbreitet hat) und nicht zuletzt und in ihrer Wirkung sicherlich am bedeutendsten die Villa der klassischen Moderne als Ergebnis einer Transformation des klassischen Typus hin zum autonomen Kunstwerk. Sowohl Mies van der Rohe als auch Le Corbusier stehen für diese Tendenz. Colin Rowe: »Darin bemerken wir ein Negieren von Volumen, ein Ersetzen durch Flächen. Dies sind Entwürfe, die als vollendete Illustration des Giedion'schen Prinzips der Raum–Zeit erscheinen, für das das Bauhaus zu Recht so berühmt ist. Es sind Kompositionen, die das Auge nicht auf einen Blick zu umfassen vermag.«[6] Diese von Colin Rowe aufgezeigte Kontraposition, dort der klassisch-monumentale Typus in Form einer symmetrisch komponierten Figur bzw. Baugruppe aus starren Körpern und hier seine modernistische Überwindung, haben die Architekturdiskussion (zu) lange blockiert bzw. in wenig fruchtbarer Weise polarisiert. Wir versuchen einen Weg zu zeigen, der herausführt aus dem starren Klassizismus und vorbei an der Unübersichtlichkeit modernistischer Kompositionen: Der Charakter des Hauses tritt in einer starken Körperform hervor und entfaltet sich als dreidimensionales, architektonisches Objekt, freistehend im eigenen Garten.

Form

Die Transformation vom Gutshaus auf dem Lande zum Bürgerhaus in der Vorstadt hat aus der Villa ein architektonisches Spielzeug für Wohlhabende gemacht; sie blieb aber zunächst der klassischen Architektursprache verhaftet, mal eher monumental, mal eher malerisch, oft schlichtweg kitschig. Erst mit der Moderne des 20. Jahrhunderts ist sie zum autonomen Kunstwerk mutiert. Beide Tendenzen, so man sie antipodisch betrachtet, sind noch ganz lebendig und der ideologische Krieg zwischen ihren Propagandisten dauert unvermindert an. Es gibt Architekten und Bauherren, die behaupten, eine Villa könne in Anbetracht ihrer heroischen Geschichte eigentlich nur klassizistisch geformt sein; die Modernisten dagegen behaupten genau das Gegenteil. Mit den hier vorgestellten Entwürfen wollen wir uns dieser Stildebatte entziehen. Wir thematisieren die Villa über die Radikalität ihrer Form als

lutionary period. There, it was a matter of effects and the spectacular, but also of a desire »for the building to speak, to announce its purpose«.[7] What was meant by that, for example, was that a cowshed should have the form of a cow. We are not interested in such ideas, but in a visually powerful architecture with a high identification value and the potential for linguistic identification. The house has a form, and even if this form is very simple, it is able to impress itself on the mind as an image and thus develop a narrative potential. When the three-dimensional manifestation of architecture becomes an image and develops from this image into a concept, it evolves an inevitable narrative potential, because a series of associations, feelings and memories ensue from every concept that is provoked or evoked by the object, and these tie the observer emotionally. »Architecture evolves, analogous to images and form, from all conceivable fields of life and human experience. Its formative potential is thus unlimited.«[8] Visually powerful or comprehensible architecture is perceived in an emotional and certainly subjective way and its effect develops without the necessity for particular stylistic effort. The effect stems from pure form, which is dominant, and this represents the full force of such architecture. In the case of the villa in green surroundings, this effect is particularly heightened, inasmuch as the house stands within a landscape setting. This setting is always a part of and a precondition to the effect of the villa and its architecture. The representational quality of the form is a contrast to the organic quality of nature, whereby the divisions of the object's surface (windows, pillars, walls, balustrades etc.), quite apart from their functional background, adopt the character of a »texture« subordinate to the cube rather than that of a »façade«. In this way, nothing distracts from the figure's effect, and the overall impression remains compact. It is a question of radical architecture that manages without any superfluous efforts of design or compositional tricks whatsoever and is able to develop its narrative potential in a poetic way within natural surroundings. Once the form has been established, everything else emerges as if of its own accord. That is also true of the ground plan concealed within such a shell.

This type of architecture beyond stylistic debate has had a number of forerunners in the history of architecture. The cited architecture of the Revolution by Ledoux, for example, points in this direction, even though a coarsened Classicism still dominated, and the architecture parlante led to some positively grotesque designs. The Villa Rotonda represented the beginning of this development; in stylistic terms, Schinkel's Romantic Classicism was completely tied to a rather sentimental »Italianità« by comparison, whereby the architectural volumes were picturesquely grouped in the garden. Taking up the formal radicalisation in the architecture of the Revolution, Modernism – albeit in the shadow of the dominant tendencies described as Cubist by Colin Rowe – produced some masterpieces of radical form: the Casa Malaparte (»Never say 'Villa Malaparte'. He hated the word 'villa'. For him this word

konkretes dreidimensionales Bild, das uns unmittelbar anspricht und (oder gerade weil es) sich begrifflich konkretisieren lässt. Die Form impliziert einen Namen für das Haus bzw. beim Anblick des Hauses fällt uns sofort ein Name dafür ein. Eine »architecture parlante« also? Nicht im funktionalistischen Sinne, wie sie Kaufmann in der französischen Revolutionsarchitektur sah, wo es um Effekte, um das Spektakuläre, aber auch um das Verlangen ging, »daß der Bau sprechen, von seiner Bestimmung Kunde geben soll«.[7] Gemeint war damit zum Beispiel, dass ein Kuhstall die Form einer Kuh haben soll. Nicht darum geht es, sondern um eine bildstarke Architektur mit hohem Identifikationswert und einem sprachlichen Identifikationspotential. Das Haus hat eine Form, auch wenn diese Form sehr einfach ist, kann sie sich als Bild einprägen und damit ein erzählerisches Potential entwickeln. Wenn die Architektur in ihrer dreidimensionalen Erscheinung zum Bild und vom Bild zum Begriff wird, entfaltet sie ein erzählerisches Potential deswegen, weil mit jedem Begriff, der vom Objekt provoziert oder aufgerufen wird, eine Reihe von Assoziationen, Gefühlen und Erinnerungen ihren Lauf nimmt, die den Betrachter emotional binden. »Die Architektur entfaltet sich analog zu Bildern und Gestalten aus allen möglichen Lebensbereichen und der menschlichen Erfahrung. Ihr Gestaltpotential ist somit unbegrenzt.«[8] Bildstarke bzw. begriffsfähige Architektur wird emotional und durchaus subjektiv wahrgenommen und entfaltet ihre Wirkung, ohne dass ein besonderer stilistischer Aufwand getrieben werden müsste. Es wirkt die pure Form, die dominant hervortritt, hierin liegt die ganze Stärke dieser Architektur. Im Falle der Villa im Grünen wird diese Wirkung insofern noch besonders gestärkt, als das Haus in einer landschaftlichen Szenerie steht. Diese Szenerie ist immer Teil und Voraussetzung der Wirkung der Villa und ihrer Architektur. Die Gegenständlichkeit der Form steht im Gegensatz zur Organik der Natur, wobei die Gliederung der Oberfläche des Objekts (Fenster, Pfeiler, Wände, Brüstungen usw.) abgesehen von ihrem funktionalen Hintergrund mehr den Charakter einer dem Kubus übergeworfenen »Textur« und weniger den einer »Fassade« annimmt. So lenkt nichts von der Wirkung der Figur ab, der Gesamteindruck bleibt kompakt. Es handelt sich um eine radikale Architektur, die ganz ohne überflüssigen Gestaltungsaufwand und kompositorische Tricks auskommt und ihr erzählerisches Potential in natürlicher Umgebung durchaus poetisch entfalten kann. Ist die Form einmal festgelegt, ergibt sich alles Weitere quasi von selbst. Das gilt im Übrigen auch für die Grundrisse, die in einem solchen Gehäuse stecken.

Es gibt in der Architekturgeschichte eine Ahnenreihe für diese Art von Architektur jenseits der Stildebatte. Die bereits erwähnte Revolutionsarchitektur eines Ledoux etwa weist in diese Richtung, auch wenn hier noch ein vergröberter Klassizismus vorherrscht und die »architecture parlante« zu geradezu grotesken Entwürfen geführt hat. Die Villa Rotonda stand am Anfang dieser Entwicklung und der romanti-

was the quintessence of anything 'bourgeois'.«[9]) on the Island of Capri as a ramp of steps over the open sea; Konstantin Melnikow's own house in the form of a double cylinder; Le Corbusier's »Villa Savoie« as a floating box in the open countryside, which evades stylistic classification and represents pure form (at least when viewed from a distance). There are Bruno Taut's »Park Keeper's House« from 1921 and his »Monument in Iron« from 1913 – both designs being forceful examples of radical forms, although they are not villas. Or there is Mies van der Rohe's »Farnsworth House« as an extreme case of autonomous architecture, like Livio Vacchini's own house in Costa. All these projects differ in their degree of abstraction and their figurative character, certainly, but they share the unconditional emphasis of a powerful form, which surprises the observer and makes a direct impression on him.

»I refer to the quality of a building that permits it to have a marked effect on our heart as its character«, wrote an unknown author around 1788.[10] So we are concerned with characteristic buildings. The minimalist box is one possibility, but not the aim of design, and we would like to show that a morphological alteration of the form that »comes from the box« produces a large number of powerful objects, whereby the issue »with or without a roof?« (another question of faith in architecture) becomes obsolete. »The clearly outlined forms are the ones that create quite specific qualities«[11] and it is the individuality of these that meets the villa-dweller's distinct need to be able to identify himself with his house. Each of the houses shown here implies a different, very individual feeling for life.

Klaus Theo Brenner

1 Max Weber: *Wirtschaft und Gesellschaft*, Gesamtausgabe. Teilband 5: *Die Stadt*; Tübingen 1999, p. 59
2 Klaus Theo Brenner, Helmut Geisert: *Das städtische Reihenhaus*; Stuttgart 2004
3 Max Weber, op. cit., p. 67
4 Rudolf Borchardt: *Italienische Städte und Landschaften. Die Villa*; Stuttgart 1998, p. 20
5 Rudolf Borchardt, op. cit.; p. 21, 22
6 Colin Rowe: *Die Mathematik der idealen Villa und andere Essays*; Basel, Berlin, Boston, 1998, p. 52, 53
7 Emil Kaufmann: *Von Ledoux bis Le Corbusier*, Nachdruck; Stuttgart 1985, p. 30
8 Klaus Theo Brenner: *Stadttheater – Urban Theatre. Manifeste für eine stillose Architektur*; Berlin 1994, p. 57
9 Karl Lagerfeld: *Casa Malaparte*; Göttingen 1998
10 Anonym: *Untersuchungen über den Charakter der Gebäude*; Leipzig 1788,
    Faksimile-Neudruck Nördlingen 1986, p. 11
11 Donald Judd: *Spezifische Objekte in Minimal Art*; Dresden, Basel 1995, p. 59/60

sche Klassizismus Schinkels war stilistisch gesehen im Vergleich dazu noch ganz einer eher sentimentalen »Italianità« verhaftet, wo die Baukörper sich malerisch im Garten gruppieren. Anknüpfend an die Radikalisierung der Form in der Revolutionsarchitektur hat die Moderne, allerdings im Schlagschatten der von Colin Rowe bezeichneten kubistischen Haupttendenzen, einige Meisterwerke der radikalen Form hervorgebracht: die Casa Malaparte (»Never say ‚Villa Malaparte'. He hated the word ‚villa'. For him this word was the quintessence of anything ‚bourgeois'.«[9]) auf der Insel Capri als Stufenrampe über dem offenen Meer. Konstantin Melnikows eigenes Wohnhaus in Form eines Doppelzylinders. Le Corbusiers »Villa Savoie« als schwebende Kiste in offener Landschaft, die sich jeder stilistischen Klassifizierung entzieht und als reine Form dasteht (zumindest aus der Ferne betrachtet). Bruno Tauts »Parkwächterhaus« von 1921 oder sein »Monument des Eisens« von 1913 – beide Entwürfe sind starke Beispiele für radikale Formen, ohne allerdings Villenentwürfe zu sein. Mies van der Rohes »Farnsworth House«, ein Extremfall autonomer Architektur, ebenso wie Livio Vacchinis eigenes Wohnhaus in Costa. All diese Projekte sind in ihrem Abstraktionsgrad und ihrem figürlichen Charakter durchaus unterschiedlich, was sie vereint, ist das bedingungslose Hervortreten einer starken Form, die den Betrachter überrascht und unmittelbar beeindruckt.

»Die Eigenschaft eines Gebäudes, wodurch es eine merkliche Wirkung auf unser Herz thut, nenne ich seinen Charakter«, so ein unbekannter Autor um 1788.[10] Es geht also um charakteristische Gebäude. Die minimalistische Kiste ist eine der Möglichkeiten, aber nicht das Entwurfsziel, und wir wollen zeigen, dass die morphologische Veränderung der Form, die »aus der Kiste kommt«, eine große Zahl starker Objekte hervorbringt, wobei die Frage »mit oder ohne Dach?« (auch eine der Glaubensfragen der Architektur) obsolet wird. »Es sind klar umrissene Formen, die ziemlich bestimmte Eigenschaften erzeugen«[11] und deren Individualität dem ausgeprägten Bedürfnis des Villenbewohners, sich mit seinem Haus zu identifizieren, entgegenkommt. Jedes dieser hier gezeigten Häuser impliziert ein anderes, sehr individuelles Lebensgefühl.

Klaus Theo Brenner

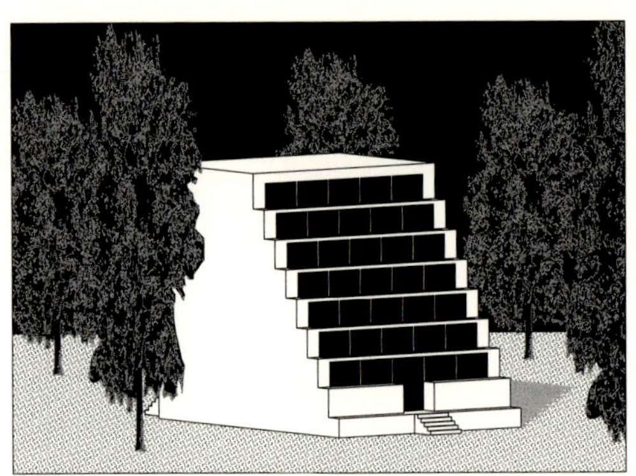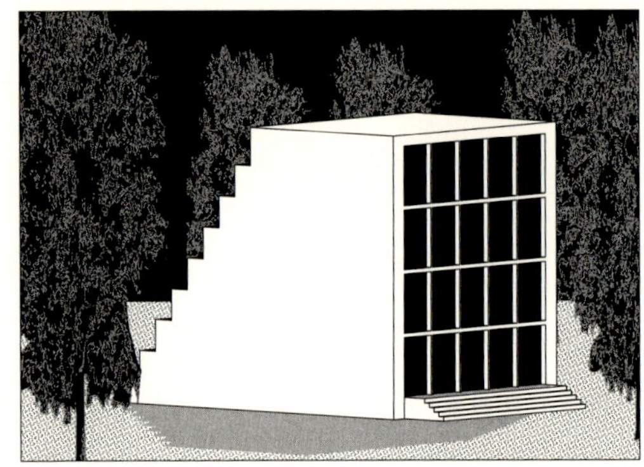

Stair House

A house like a symbol within the landscape. The sculptural appearance of this villa with its strict, formal statics conceals an interior that climbs upwards; with generous expanses of glass, its character is clearly that of a studio apartment. In a very special way, the form of this construction conveys a sense of working and living within one house, as one would expect from a studio or workshop building.

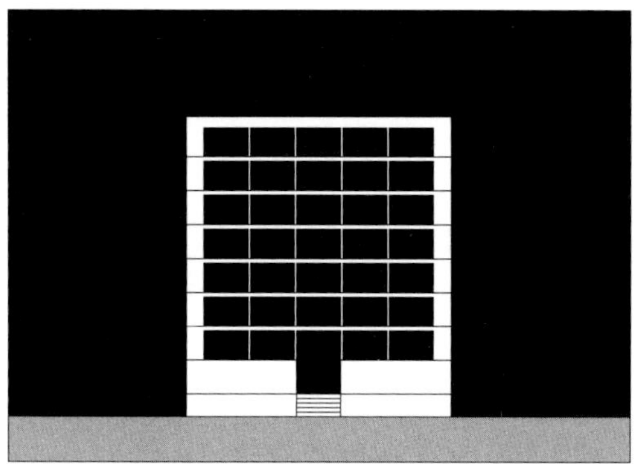 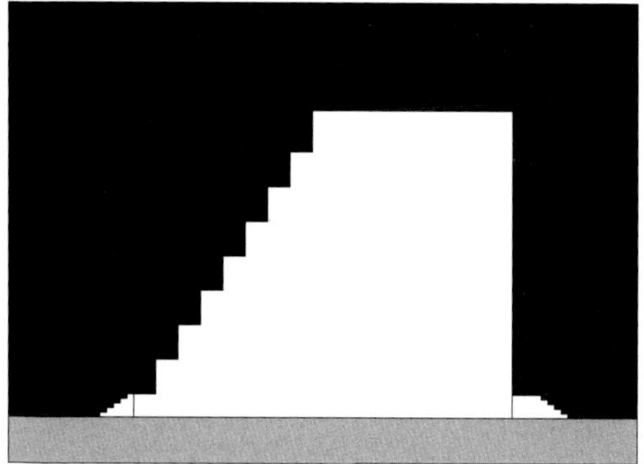

Treppenhaus

Ein Haus wie ein Zeichen in der Landschaft. Die skulpturale Erscheinungsform dieser Villa, ihre strenge formale Statik birgt einen nach oben steigenden Innenraum, der großzügig verglast den Charakter einer Atelierwohnung aufweist. In sehr spezieller Art und Weise vermittelt die Form dieses Baukörpers das Gefühl von Arbeiten und Wohnen in einem Haus, wie bei einem Atelier- oder Werkstattgebäude.

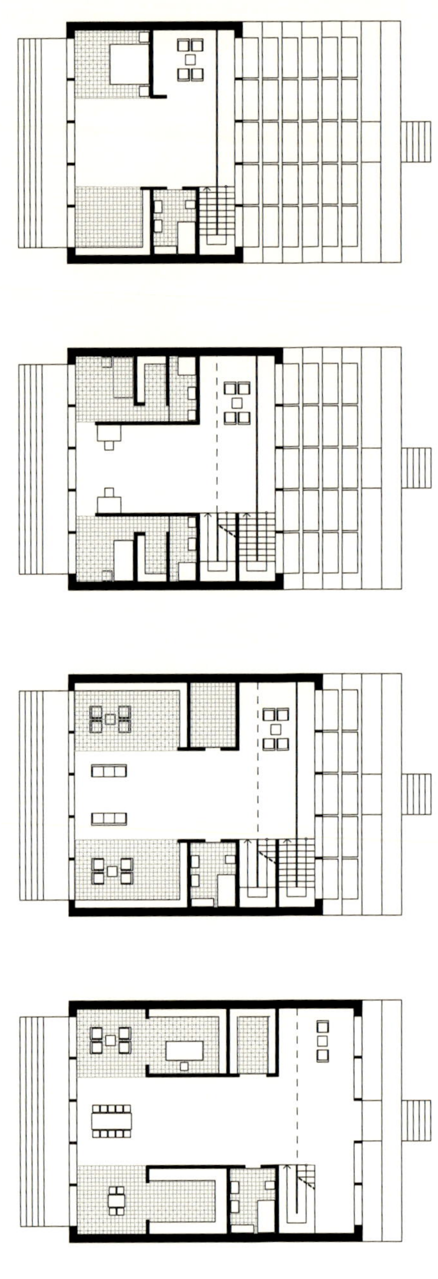

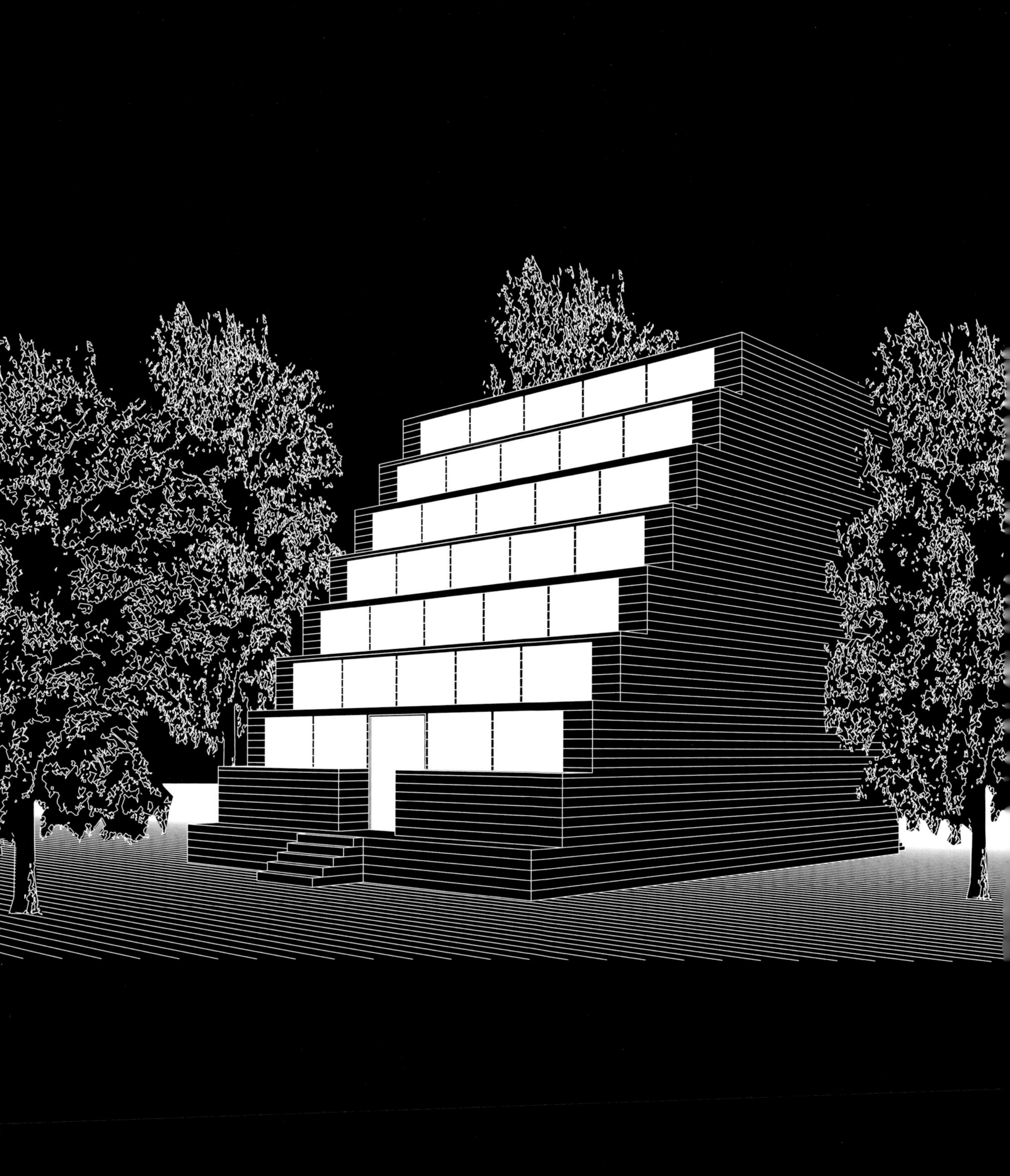

Round House

Actually, the round is a settlement form – people live in a circle, and this circle also represents the boundary to the outside world. In analogy to this, a house is a hermetically enclosed world, yet at the same time one can look out in all directions. The roof terrace would be the perfect viewing platform and an attractive living space.

Rundling

Der Rundling ist eigentlich eine Siedlungsform – man wohnt im Kreis und dieser Kreis stellt gleichzeitig die Begrenzung nach außen dar. Ein Haus ist analog dazu wie eine hermetisch abgeschlossene Welt, gleichzeitig kann man nach allen Richtungen hinausschauen. Die Dachterrasse wäre die perfekte Aussichtsplattform und ein attraktiver Lebensraum.

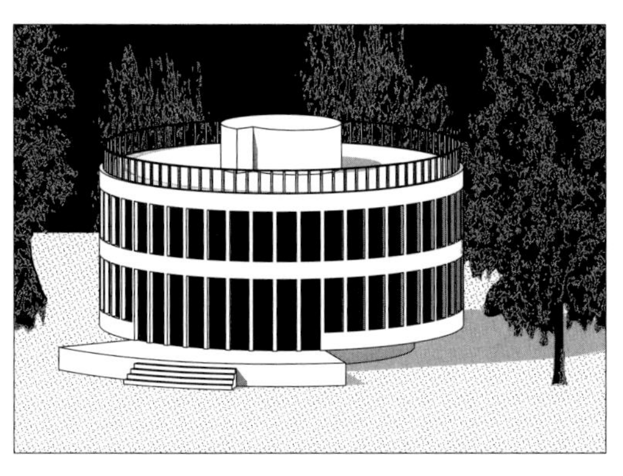
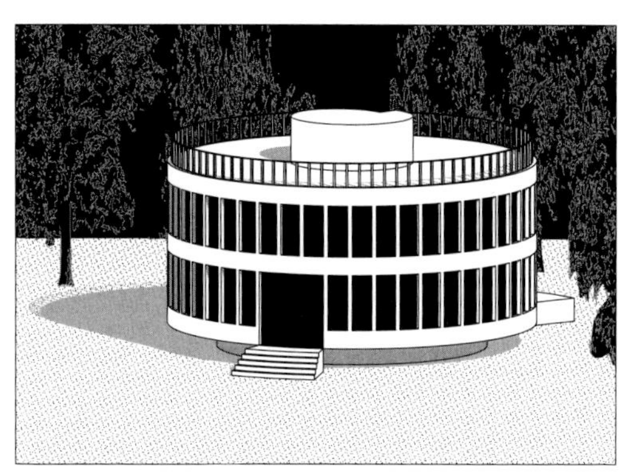
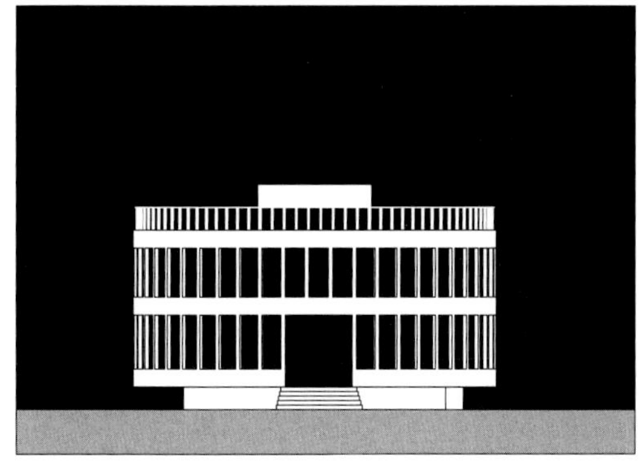
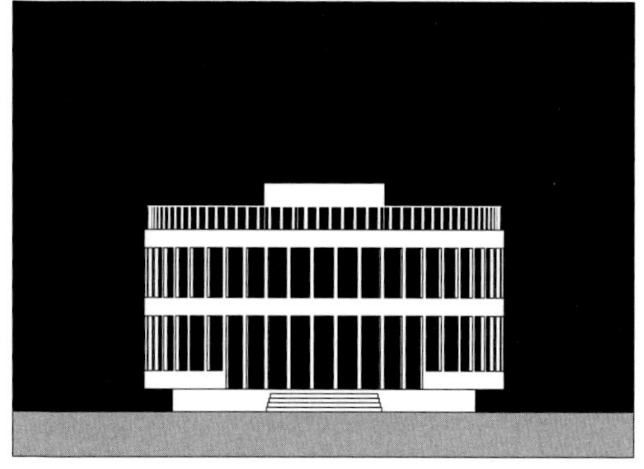

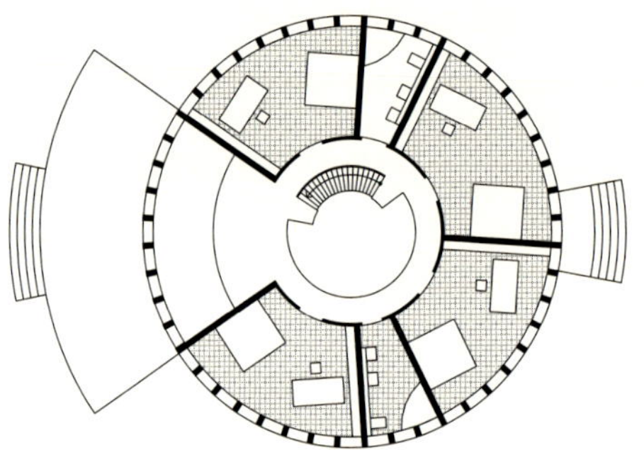

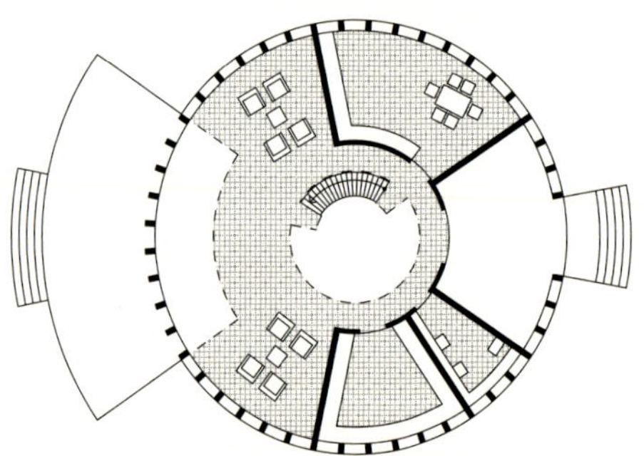

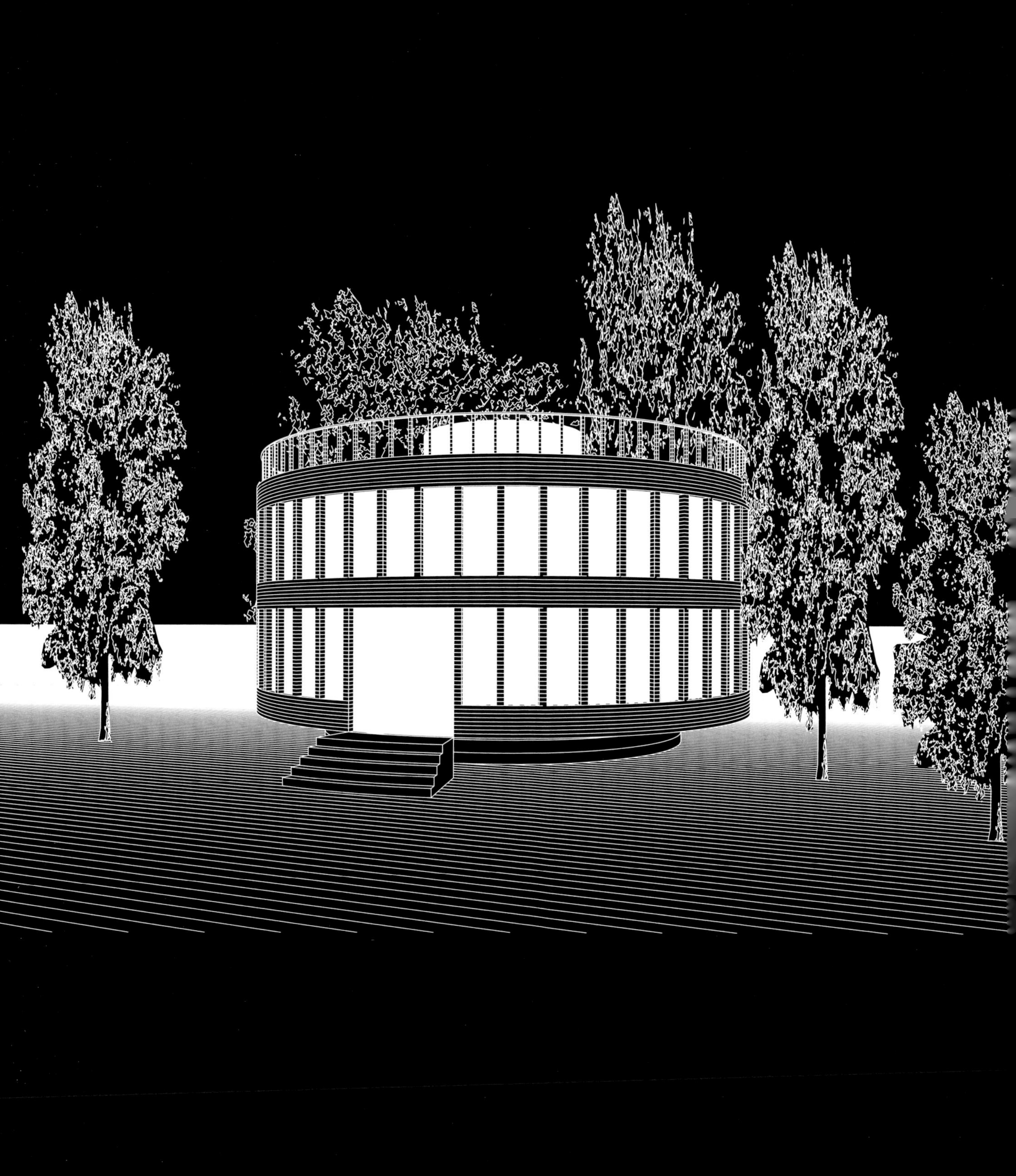

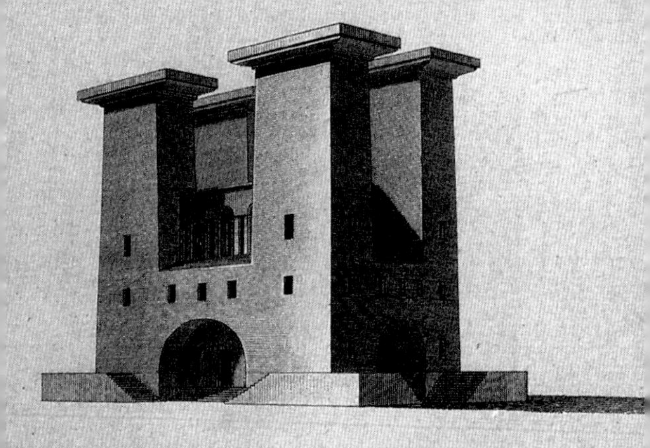

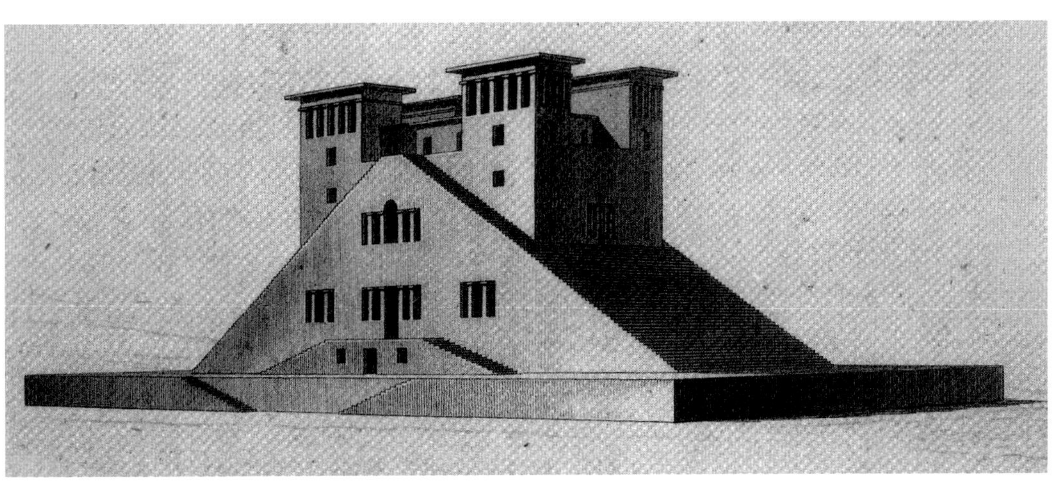

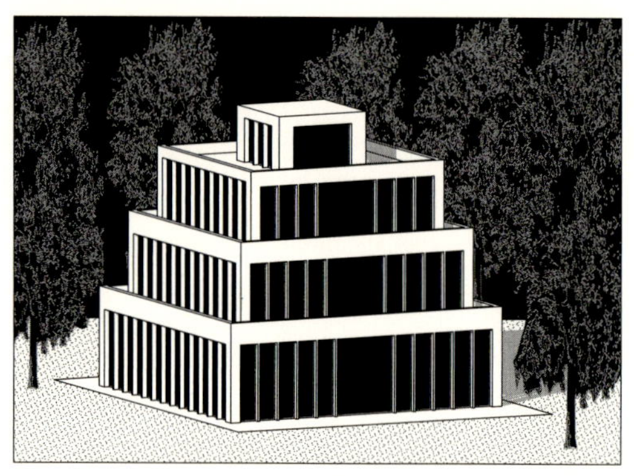 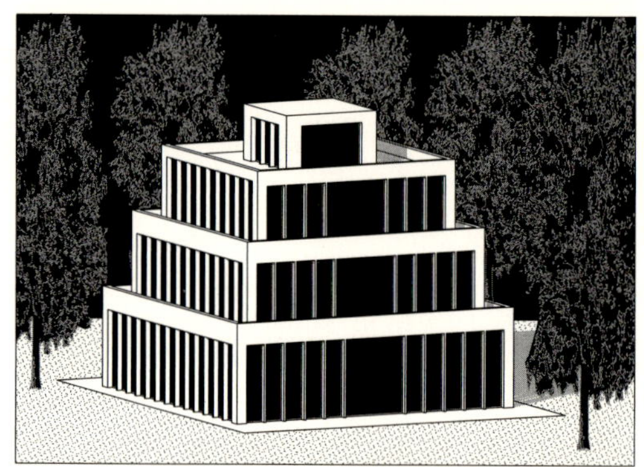

Ziggurat

The stepped pyramid can be read as both an architectonic archetype and an elementary stacking form. The quality of the interior living spaces changes, following the stacks, the further one is from the ground. The external appearance as a pyramid and the effect this has on the viewer is dependent on the materiality of the surface and the degree to which it is opened by windows.

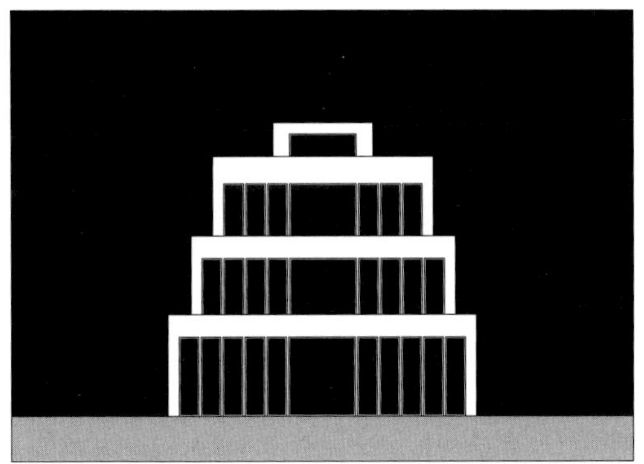 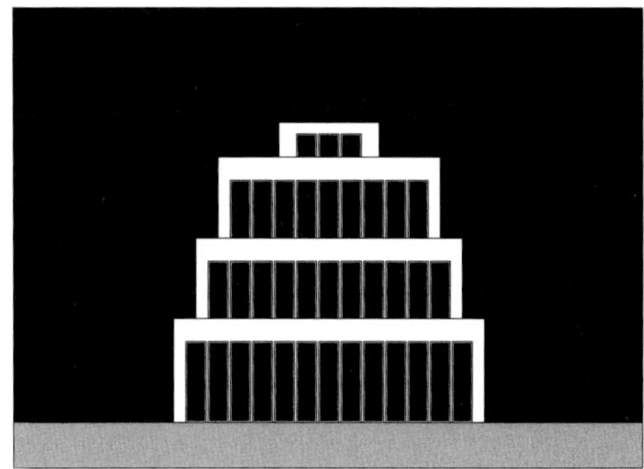

Zikkurat

Die Stufenpyramide kann man ebenso als architektonischen Archetypus wie auch als eine elementare Stapelform lesen. Die Qualität der Wohnräume im Inneren verwandelt sich, der Stapelung folgend, mit zunehmender Entfernung vom Erdboden. Die äußere Erscheinung als Pyramide und ihre Wirkung auf den Betrachter ist stark abhängig von der Materialität der Oberfläche und dem Grad ihrer Öffnung durch Fenster.

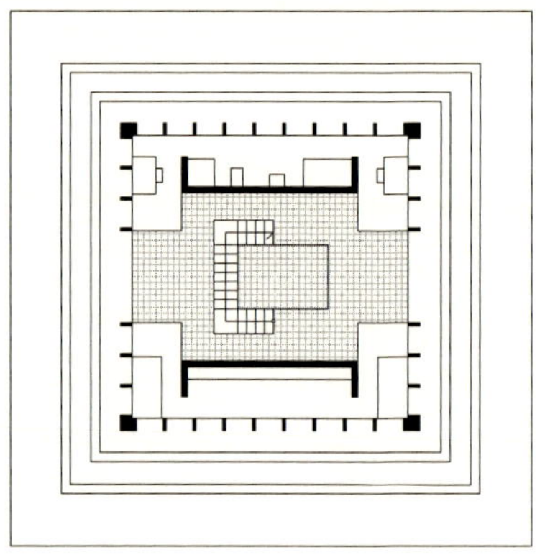

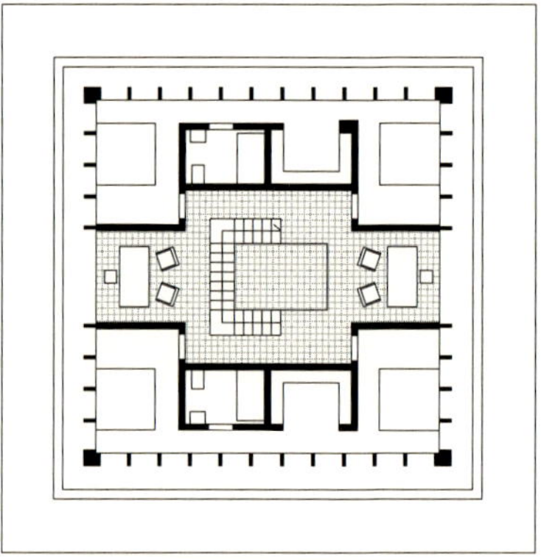

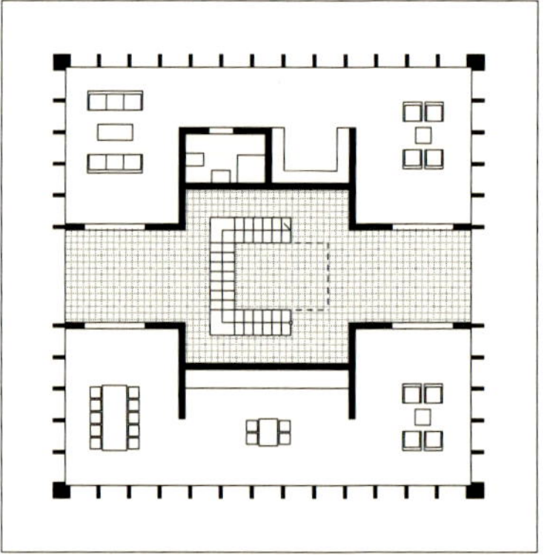

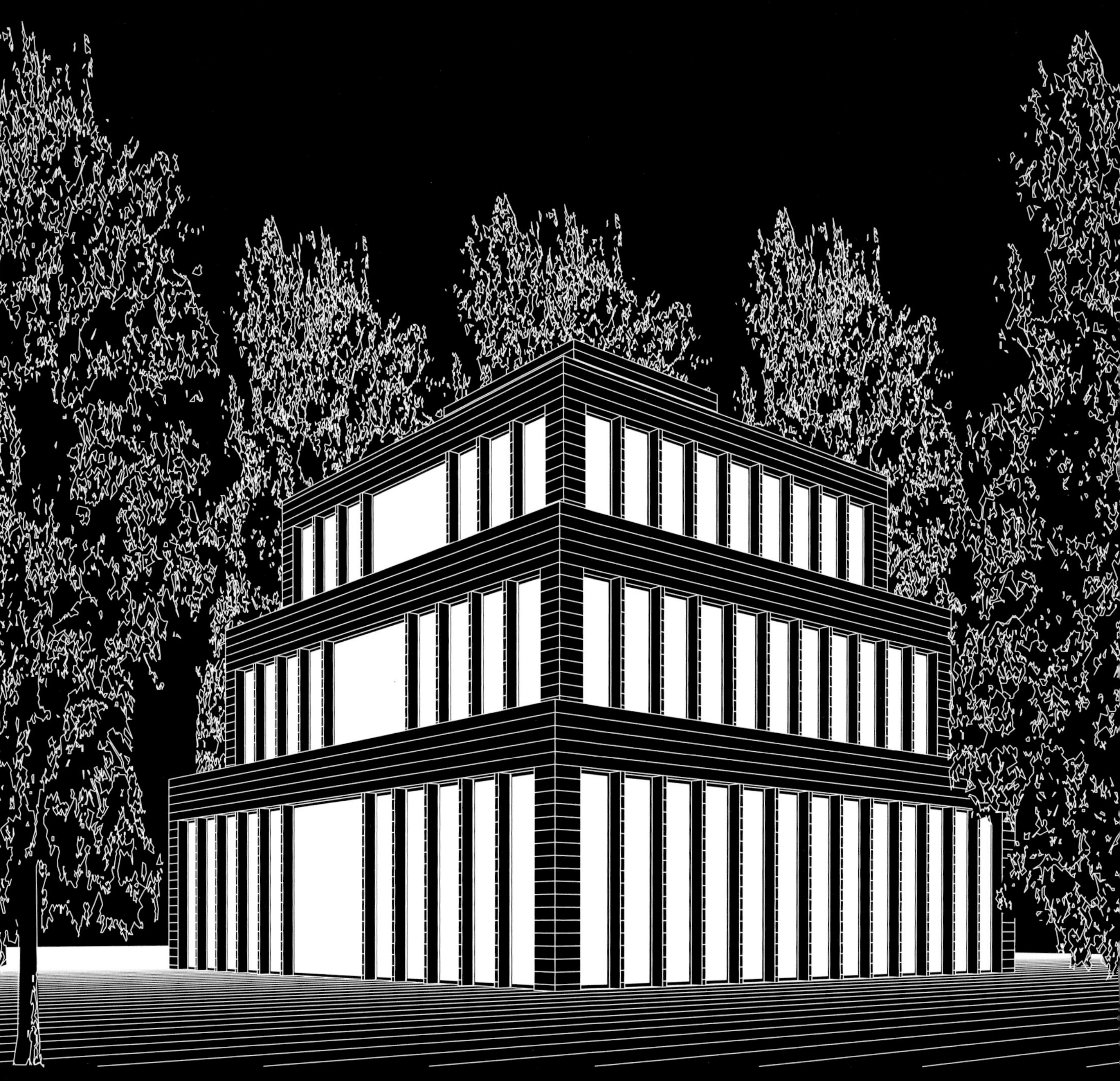

Cube

The cube house stands on a plinth like a monument; its minimalist design is demonstrated by regular openings on five sides. The rhythmic perforation of the surfaces and the interior rooms' orientation to all sides lend a certain measure of transparency to the structure's hermetic form.

Würfel

Das Würfelhaus steht wie ein Monument auf einem Sockel; seine minimalistische Gestaltung zeigt sich in regelmäßigen Öffnungen auf fünf Seiten. Die rhythmische Perforation der Oberflächen und die allseitige Orientierung der Innenräume verleiht der hermetischen Form des Baukörpers ein gewisses Maß an Transparenz.

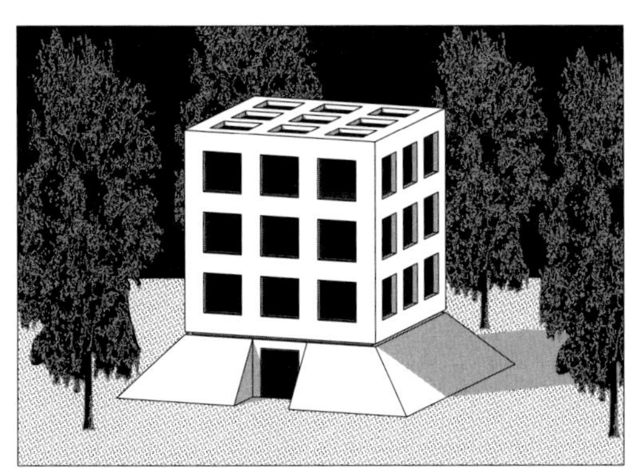
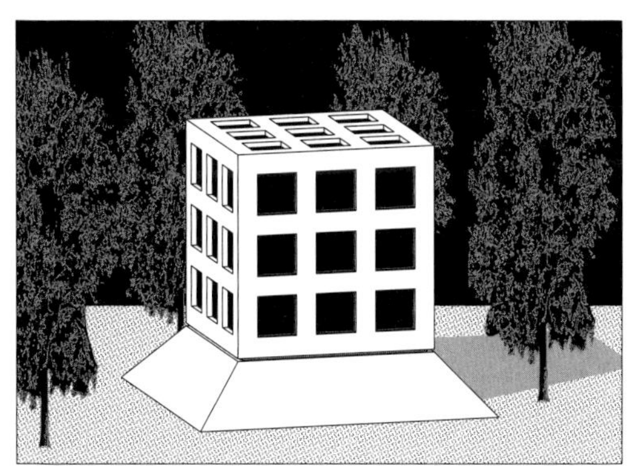
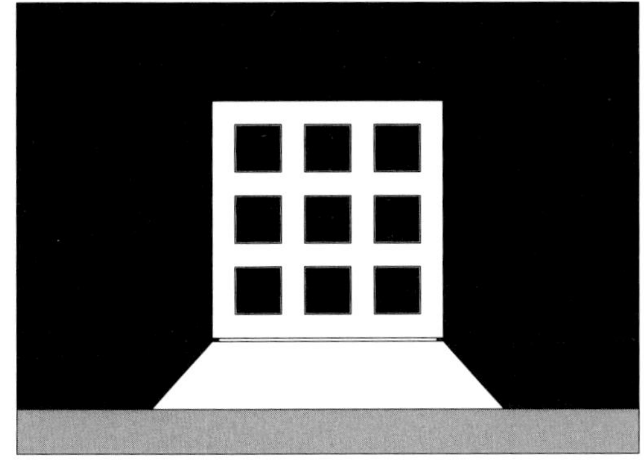
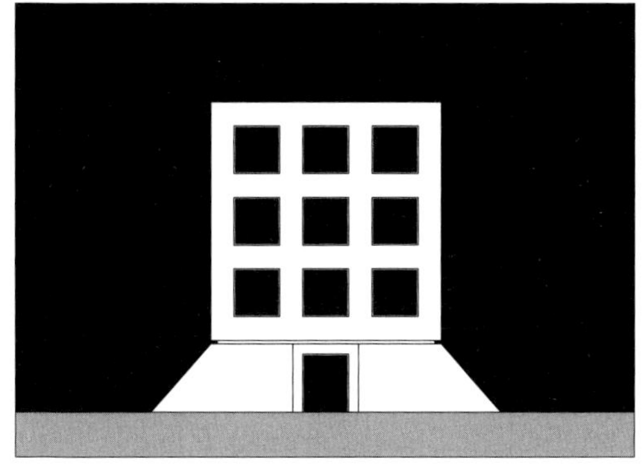

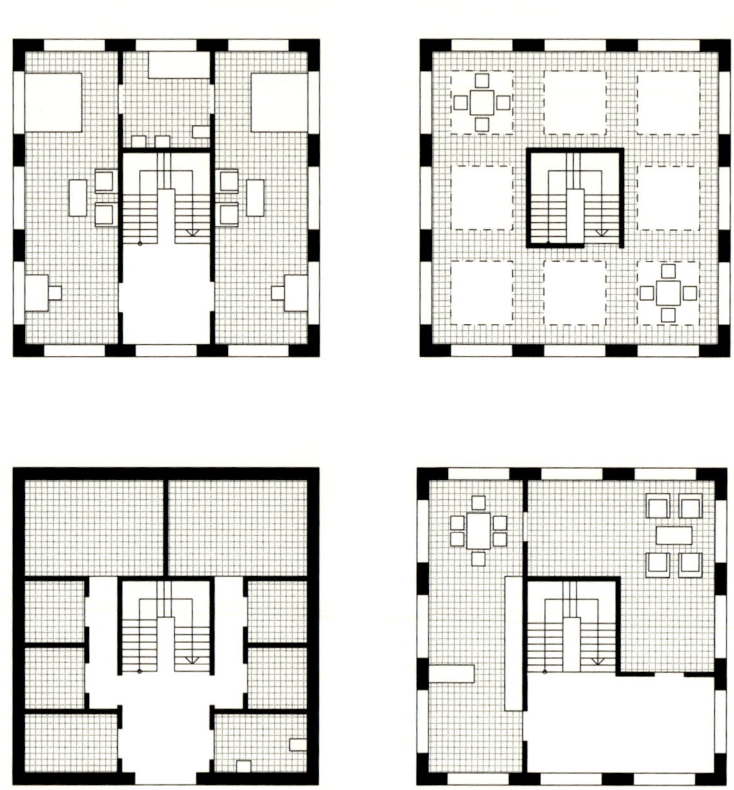

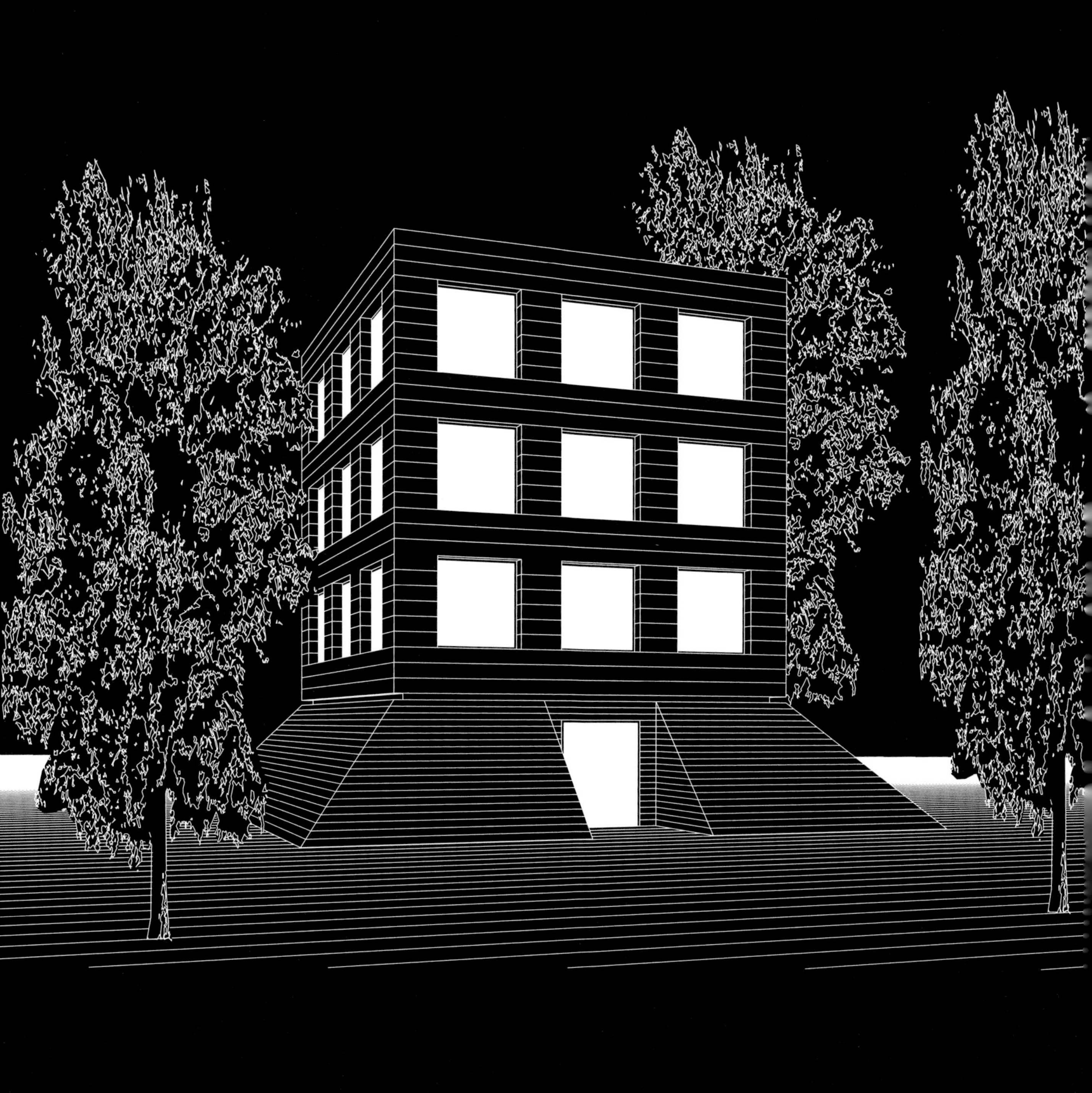

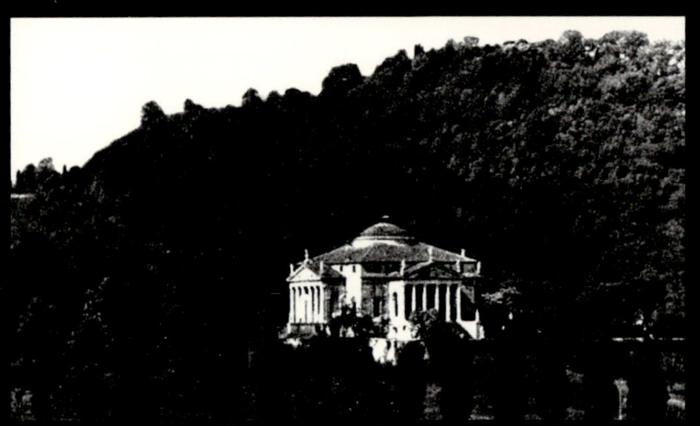

Abb. 3, 4

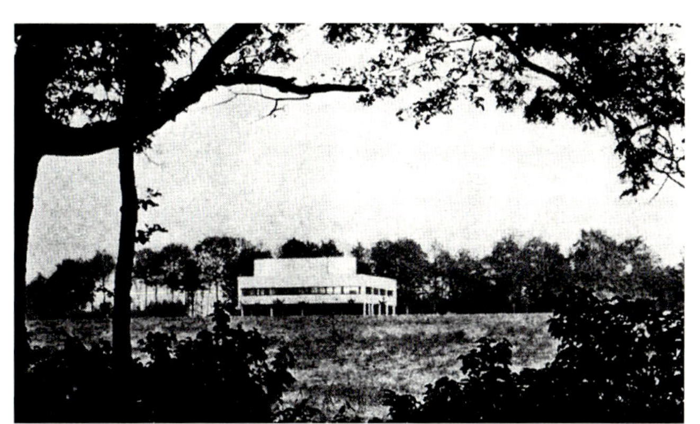

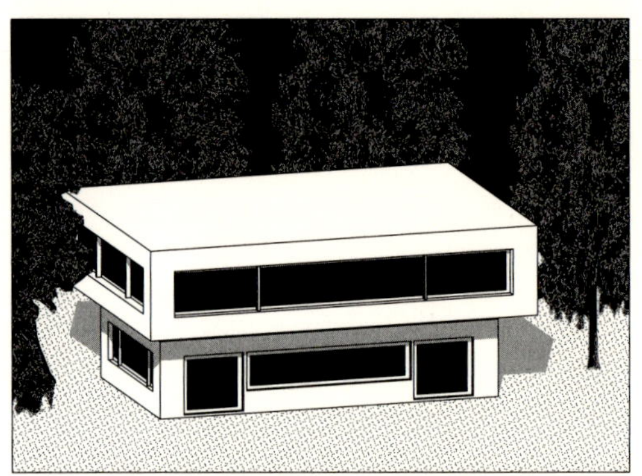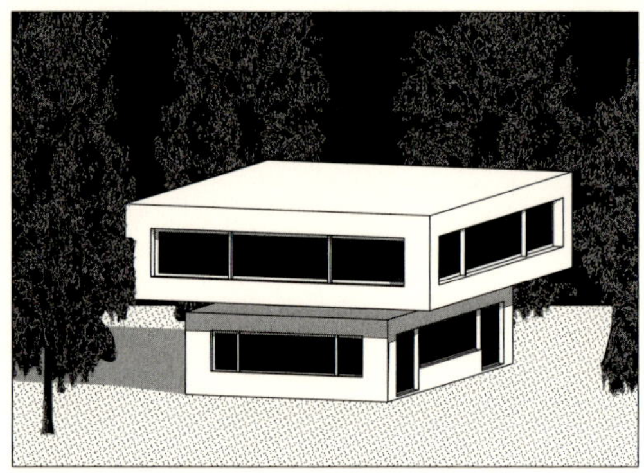

Floating House

It was a dream of Modernism to construct a house opposing the laws of gravity, or at least one that gave the impression that it was possible to do so. The consequence of such efforts is a plateau of living space resembling an observation platform. The view towards this house is also impressive, since it seems to be floating between the trees.

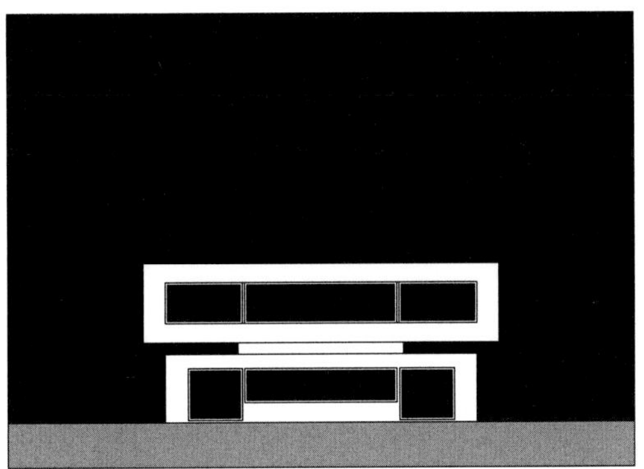 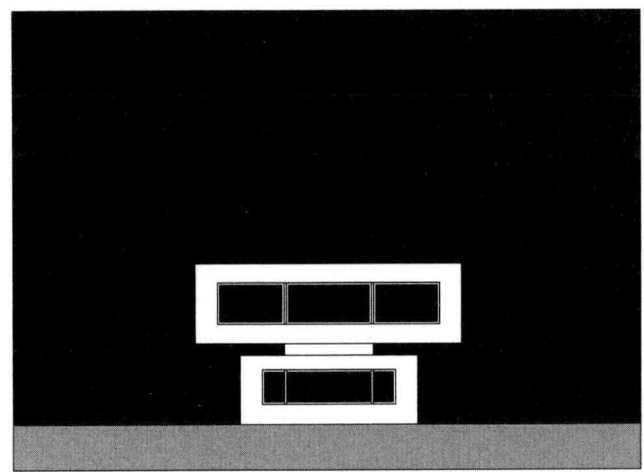

Schwebendes Haus

Ein Traum der Moderne war es, ein Haus gegen die Gesetze der Schwerkraft zu bauen oder wenigstens den Anschein zu erwecken, dass das gelingen könnte. Die Konsequenz dieser Anstrengung ist ein Wohngeschoss wie eine Aussichtsplattform. Eindrucksvoll ist auch der Blick auf ein solches Haus, das zwischen den Bäumen zu schweben scheint.

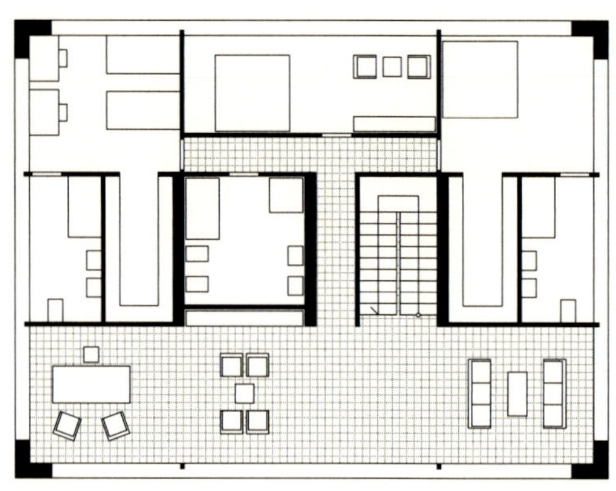

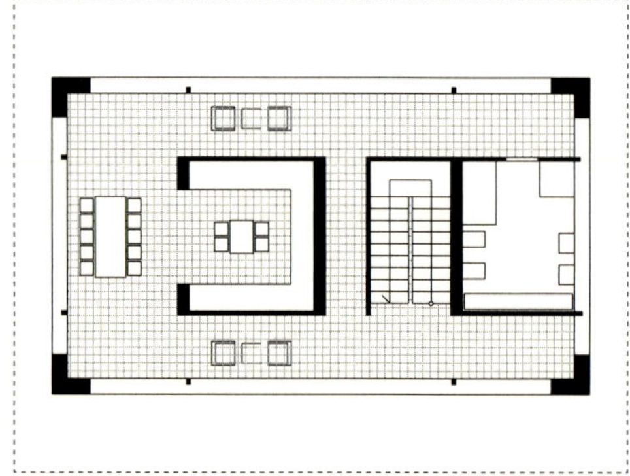

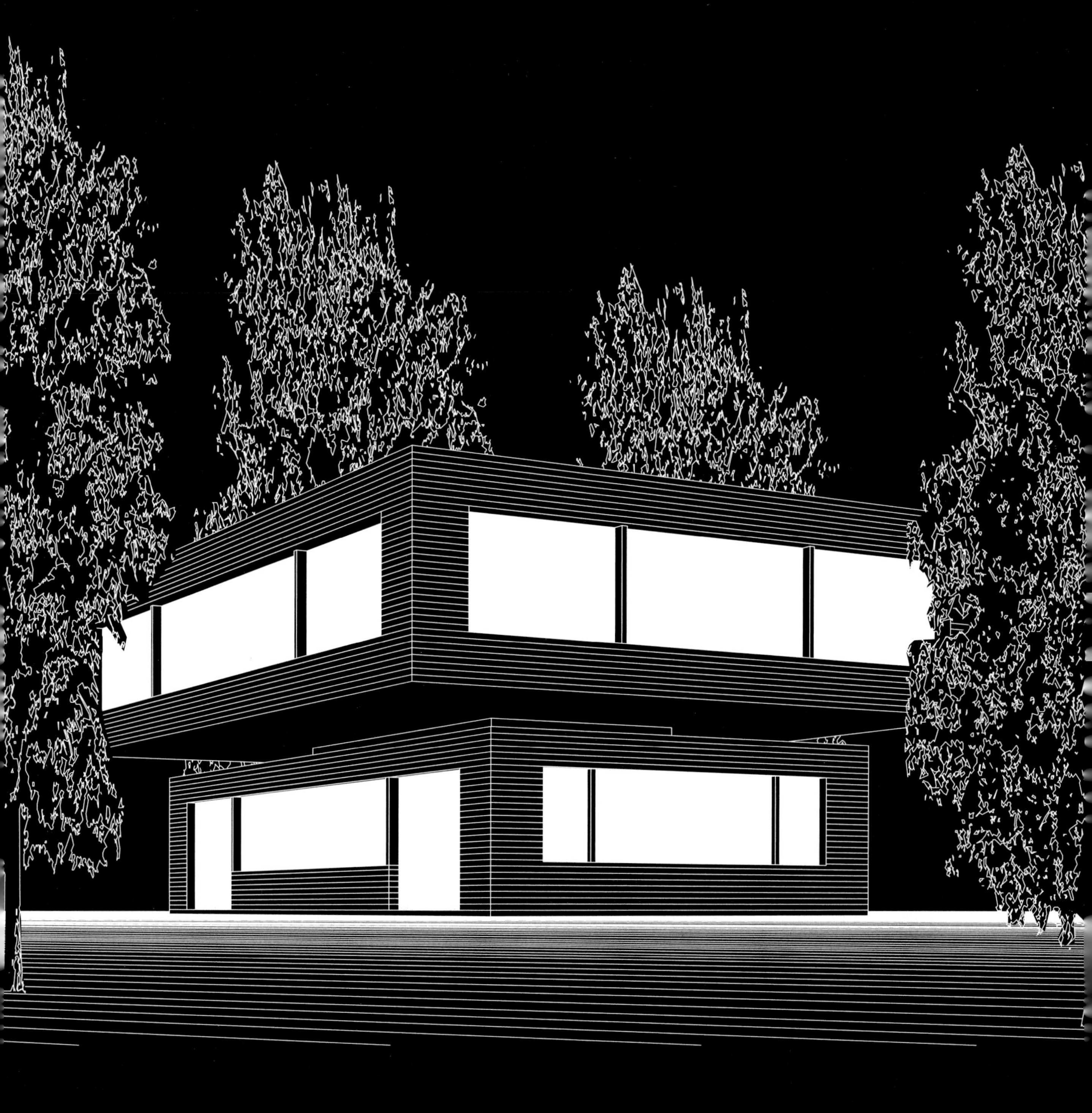

Tower

The tower, narrow as a lighthouse or watch tower, rises from an underground atrium and its living spaces are stacked above each other. An architectonic constellation for two extremely contrasting spheres within a single house; spheres that complement each other to create an individual way of life.

Turm

Der Turm erhebt sich schlank wie ein Leuchtturm oder Wachturm mit übereinander gestapelten Wohnräumen aus einem unterirdischen Atrium heraus. Eine architektonische Konstellation für zwei extrem gegensätzliche Lebenssphären in einem Haus, die sich zu einer individuellen Lebensform ergänzen.

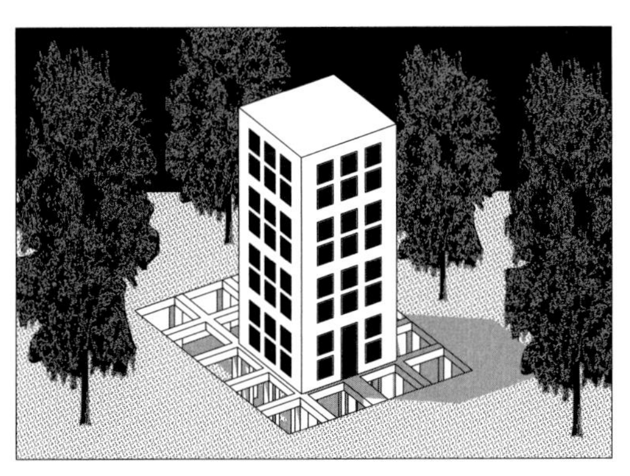
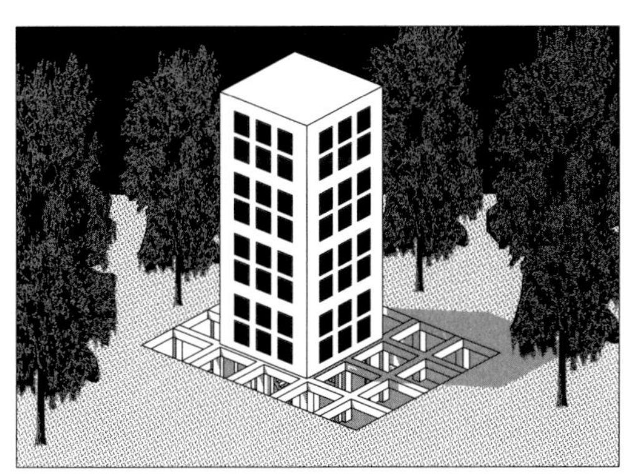
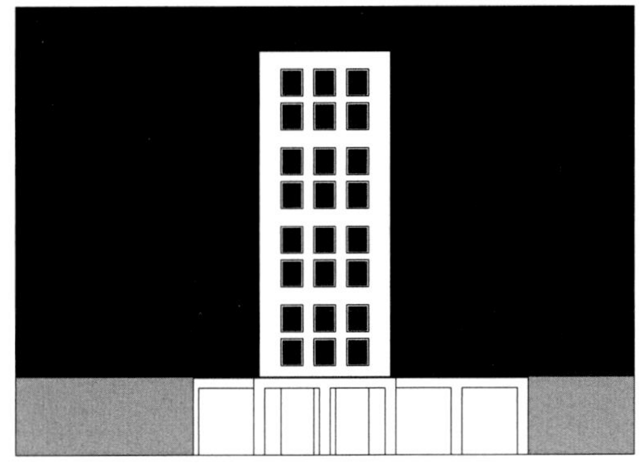
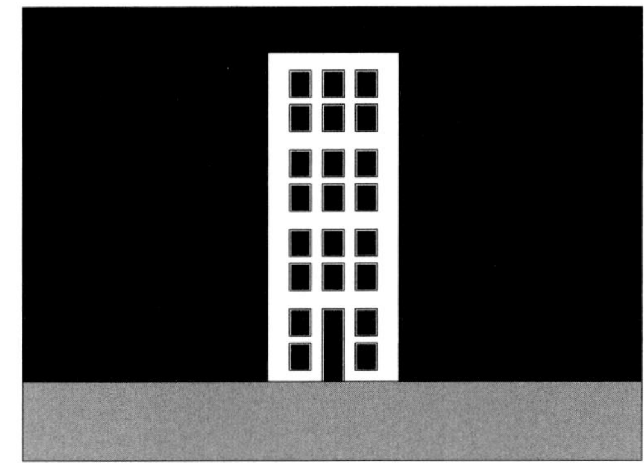

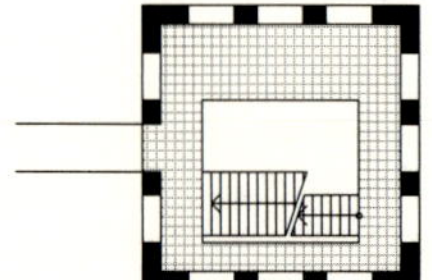
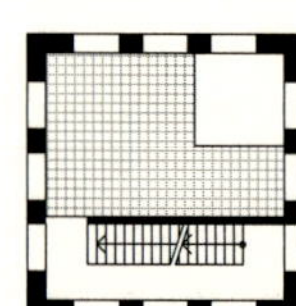
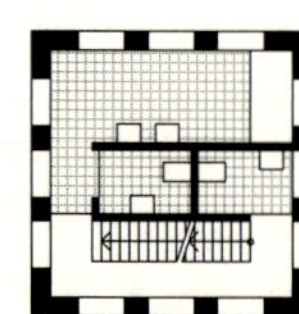
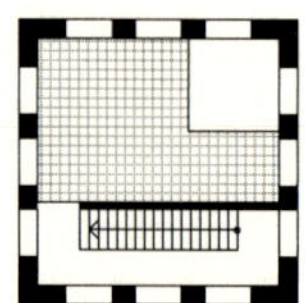
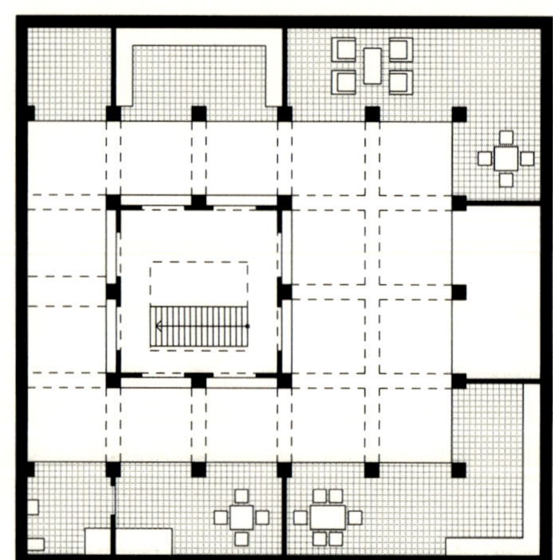

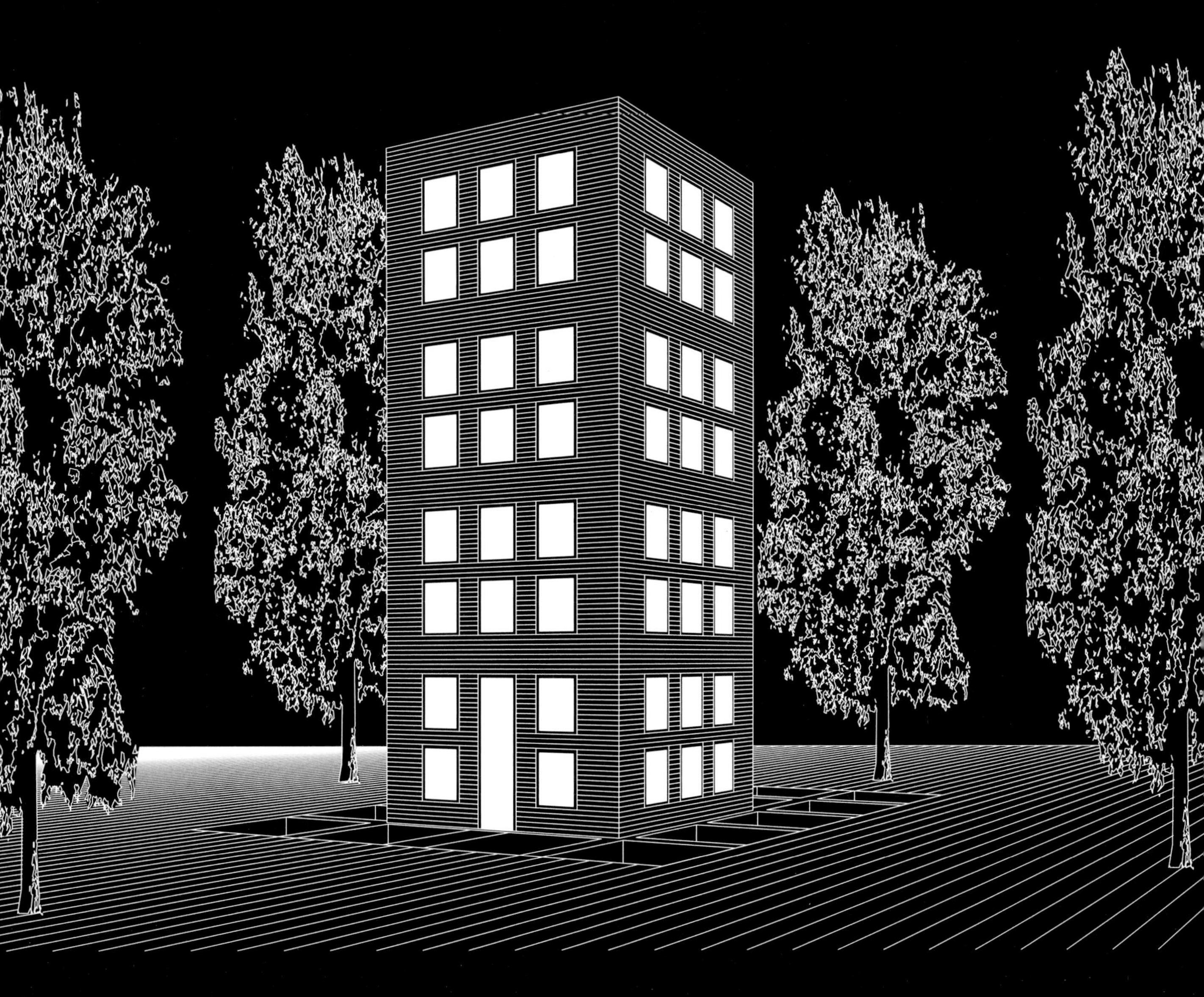

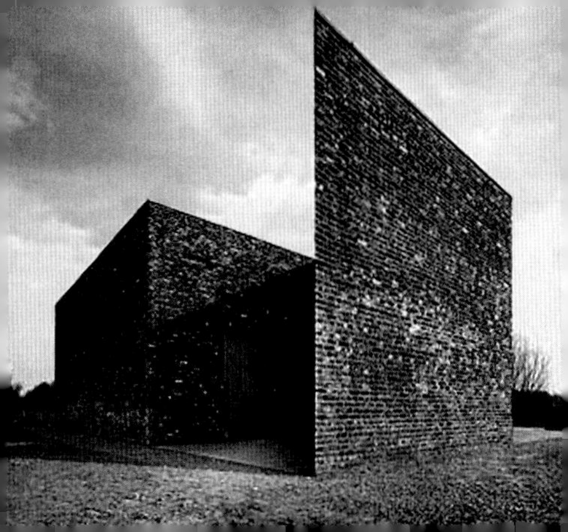

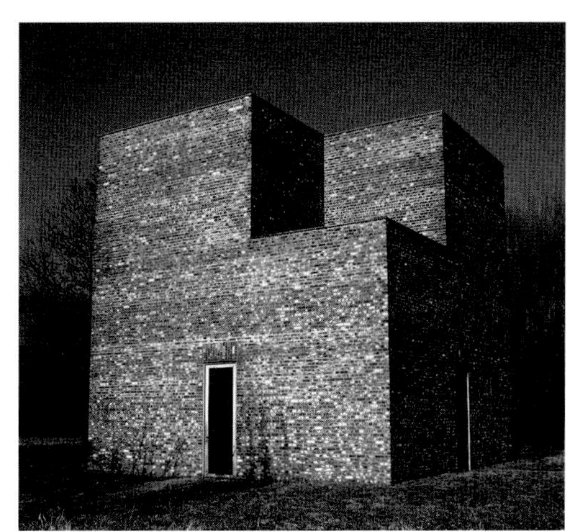

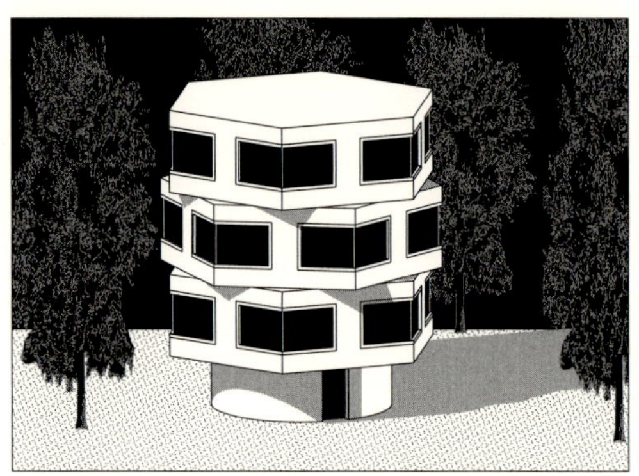 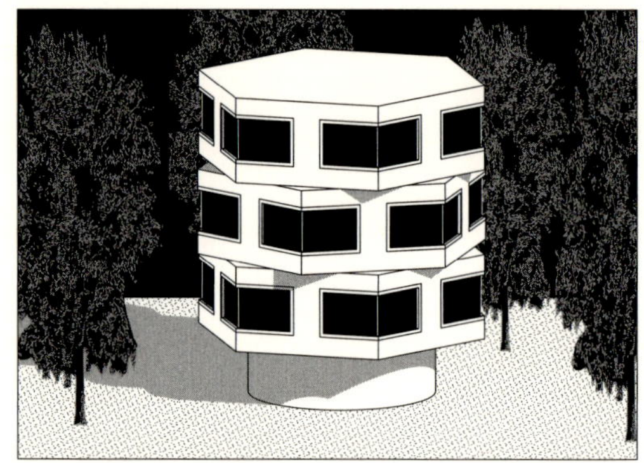

Screw

The attraction of this laconic project lies in the very simple addition – or rather distortion – of a six-sided block. The result is a tower-like house with special characteristics. Villa architecture in particular offers a field of experiment in which to adapt elementary forms other than the classical vocabulary and to exercise a certain playful humour regarding form and effect. The »screw« is only one example of this design strategy.

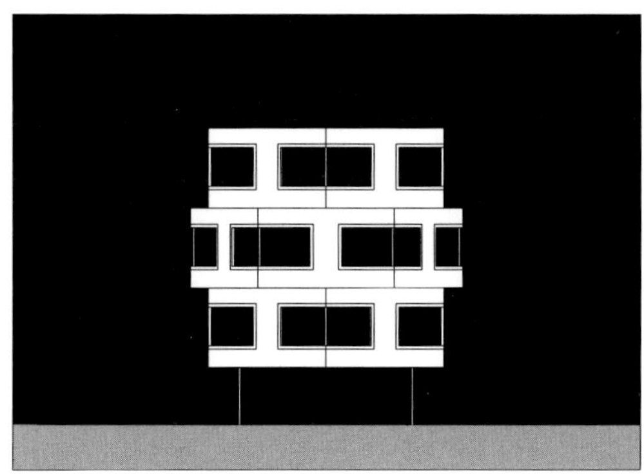 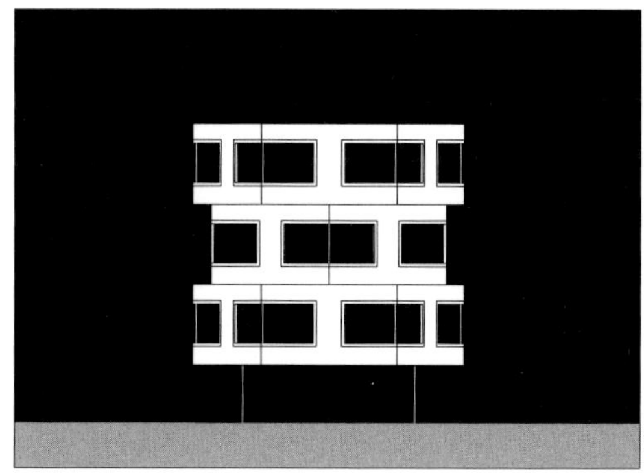

Schraube

Der Reiz dieses lapidaren Projekts liegt in seiner sehr simplen Addition bzw. Verdrehung einer Sechseck-Scheibe mit dem Ergebnis eines turmähnlichen Hauses mit besonderen Charaktereigenschaften. Gerade die Villenarchitektur bietet ein Spielfeld für Experimente mit Formen außerhalb des klassischen Vokabulars mit elementaren Qualitäten und einem gewissen spielerischen Witz in Form und Wirkung. Die »Schraube« ist nur ein Beispiel für diese Entwurfsstrategie.

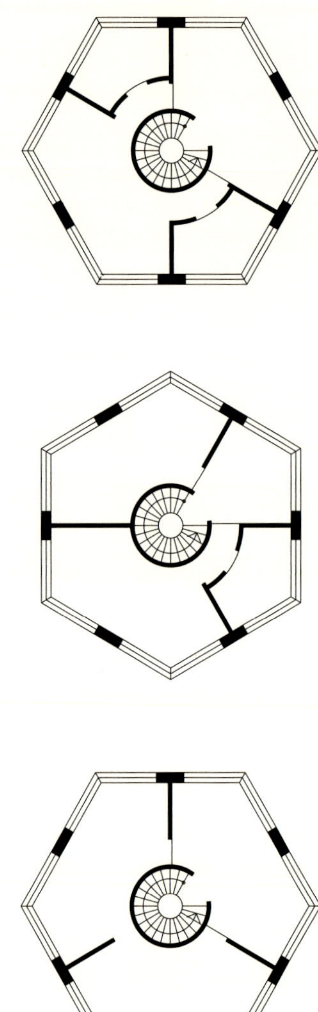

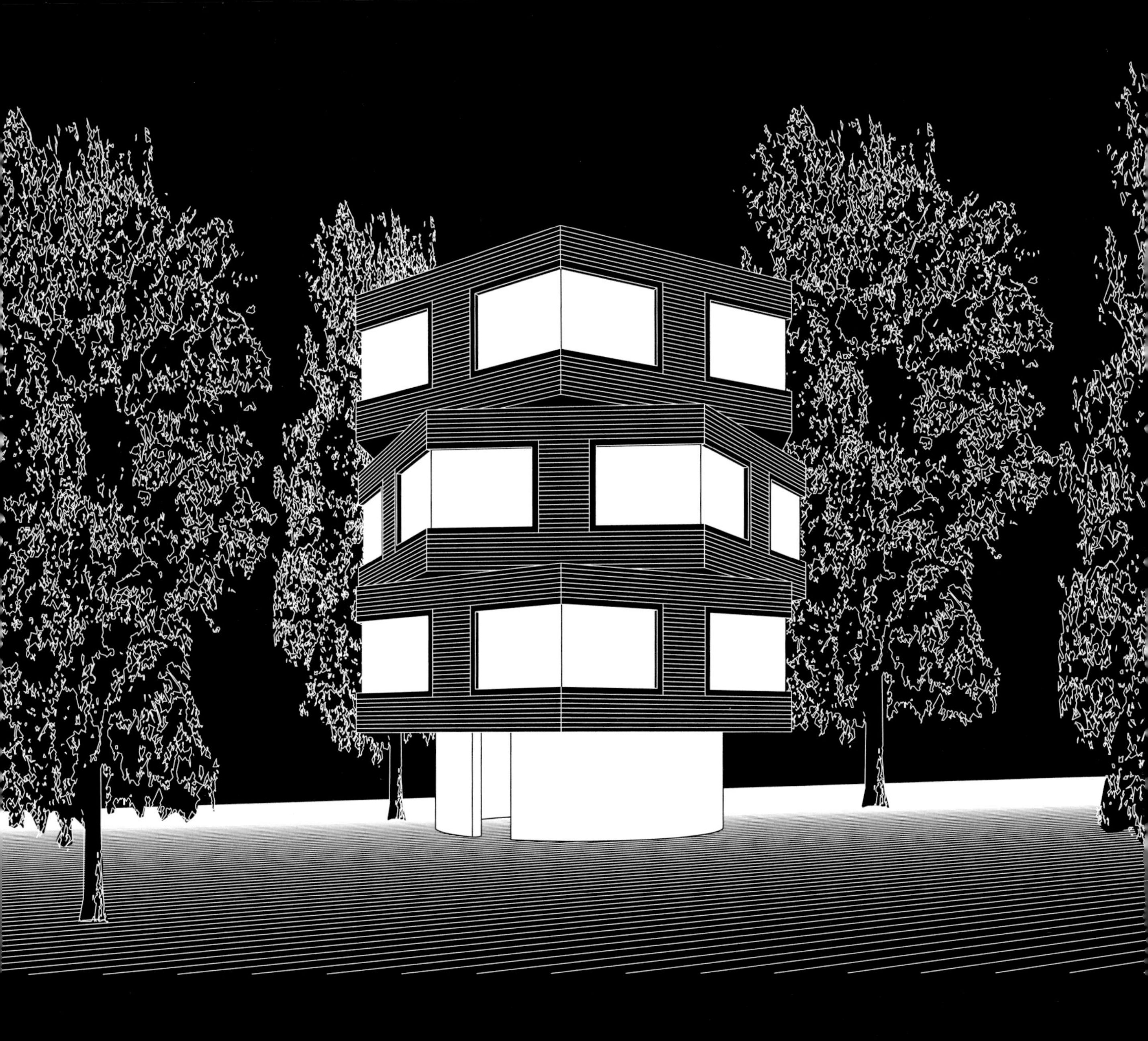

Labyrinth
A characteristic of the labyrinthine in architecture is intricacy, at least at first glance.
In the architectural object, this intricacy is achieved through a quasi Cubist deformation of the structure, which creates a differentiated constellation of individual, stag-
gered groups of rooms in the interior.

Labyrinth
Ein Wesenszug des Labyrinthischen in der Architektur ist seine Unübersichtlichkeit,
zumindest auf den ersten Blick. Diese Unübersichtlichkeit wird im architektonischen
Objekt durch eine quasi kubistische Deformation des Baukörpers erreicht, die in
ihrer Konsequenz im Inneren des Hauses ein differenziertes Gefüge von individuellen,
zueinander versetzten Raumgruppen schafft.

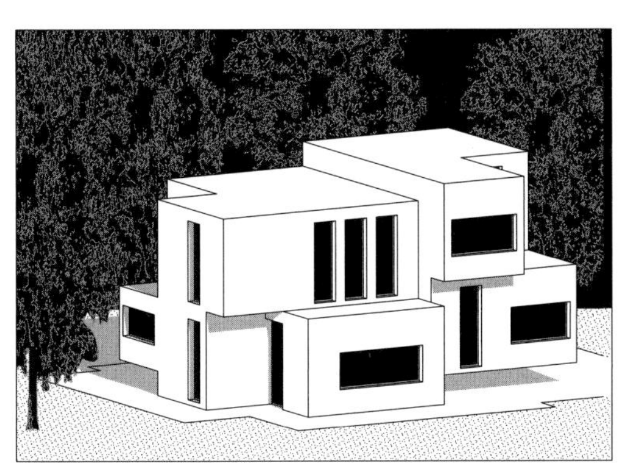
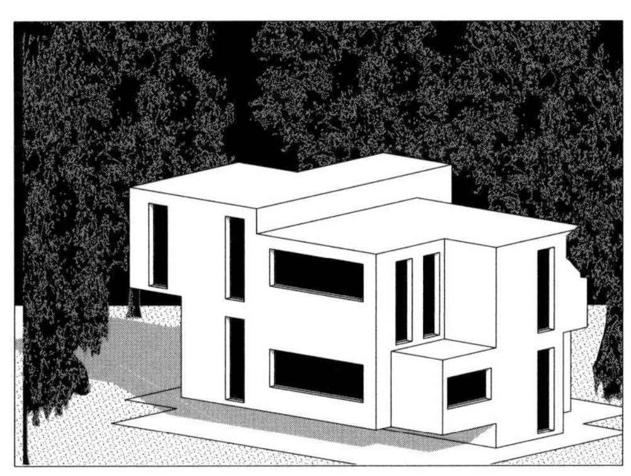
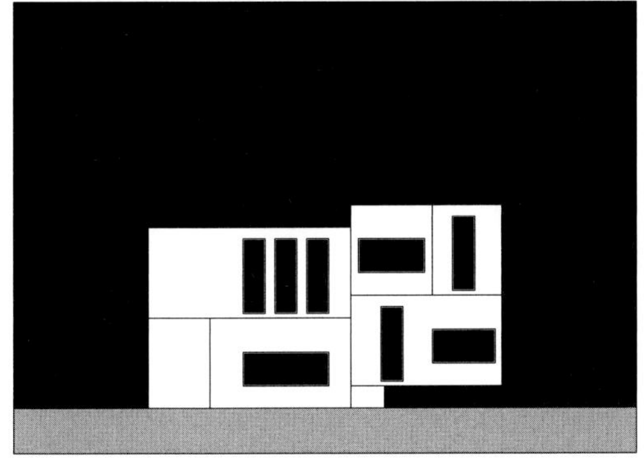
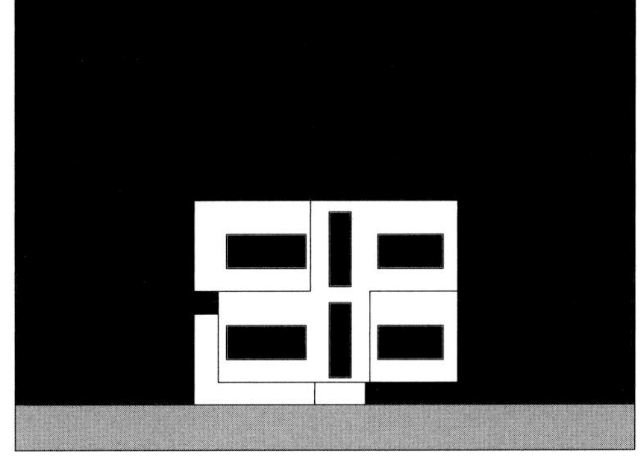

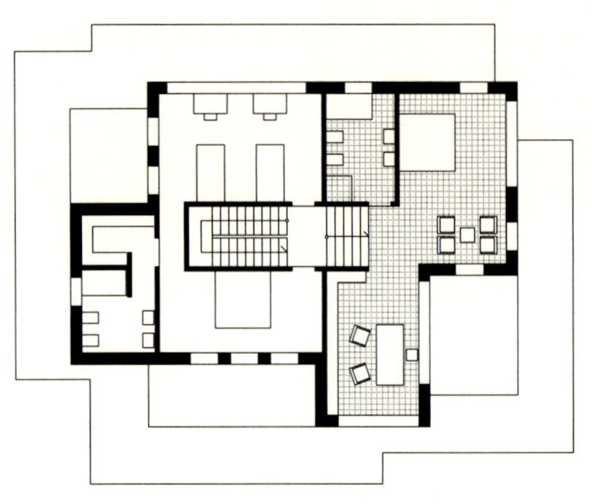

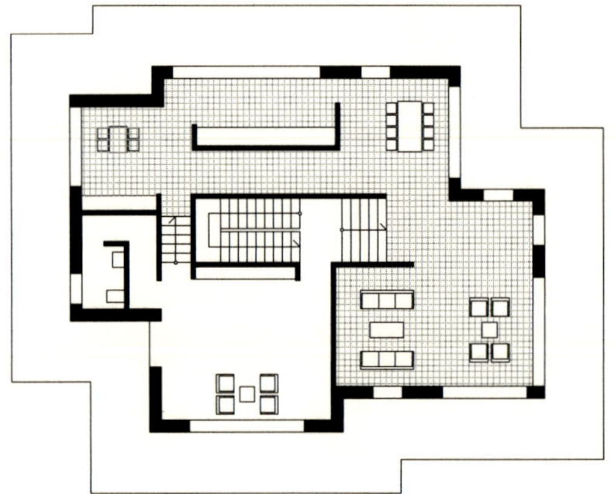

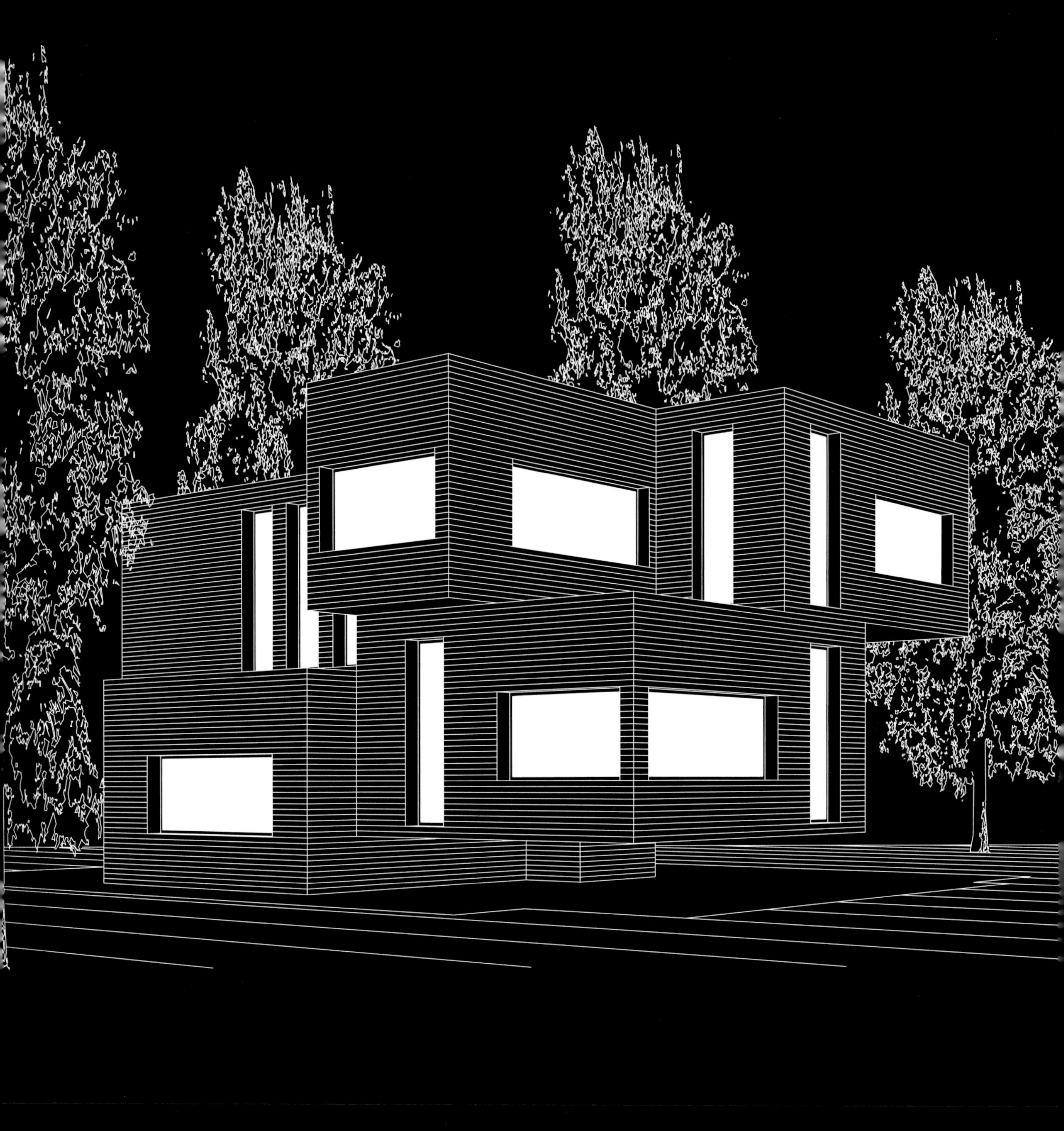

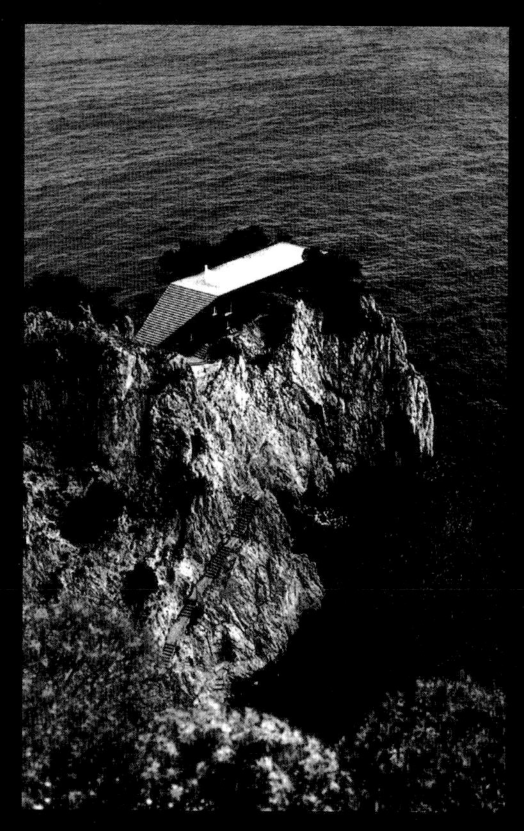

Abb. 7, 8

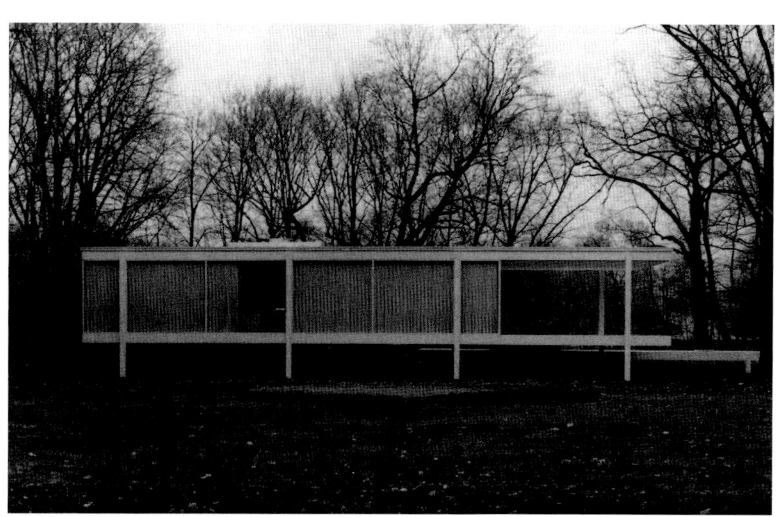

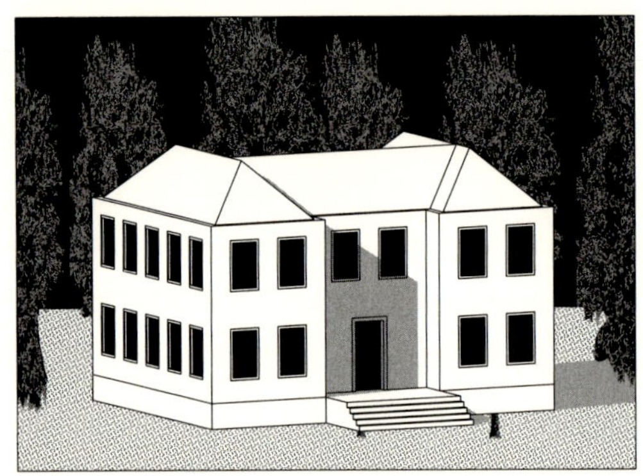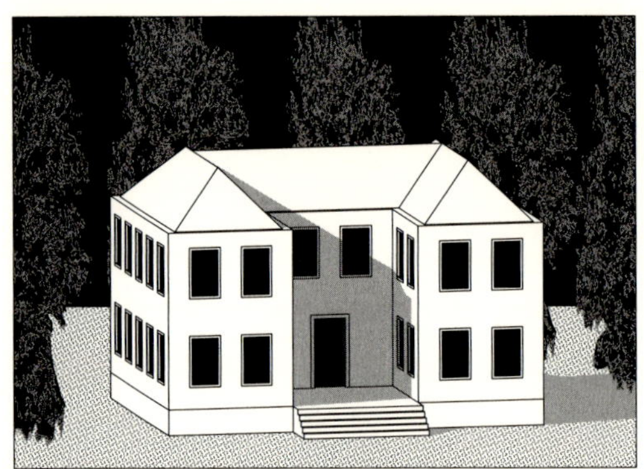

Courtyard House

The courtyard house represents the archetypal, classical villa architecture with an entrance- and garden-courtyard. The symmetry of the architectural form also characterises the organisation of the interior; this is a house gaining its full effect from the familiarity of its appearance and a certain comfort in remembering.

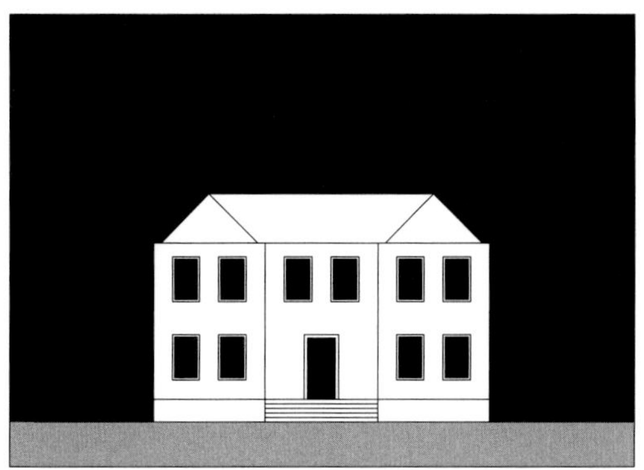 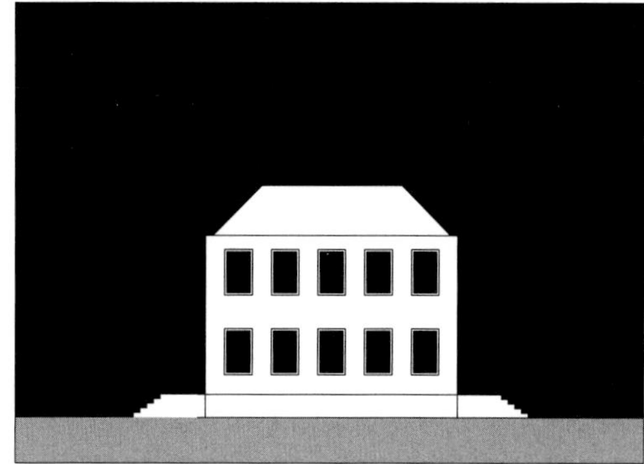

Hofhaus

Das Hofhaus steht als Archetypus für die klassische Villenarchitektur mit Eingangs- und Gartenhof. Die Symmetrie der baulichen Figur ist prägend für die Organisation des Innenlebens in einem Haus, das seine Wirkung ganz aus der Vertrautheit des Bildes und einer gewissen Behaglichkeit im Erinnern bezieht.

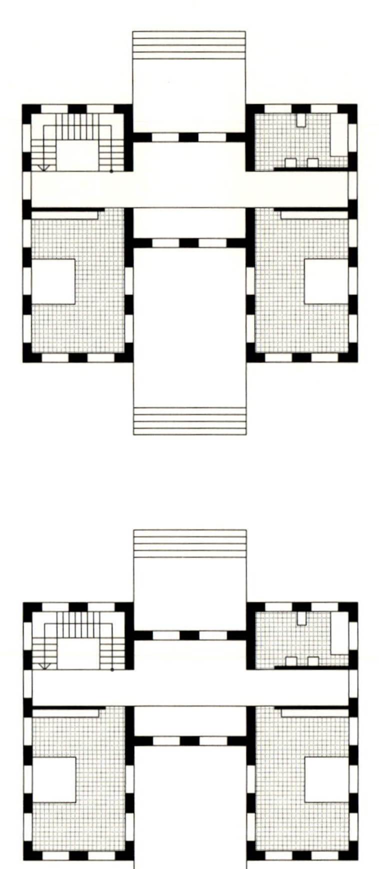

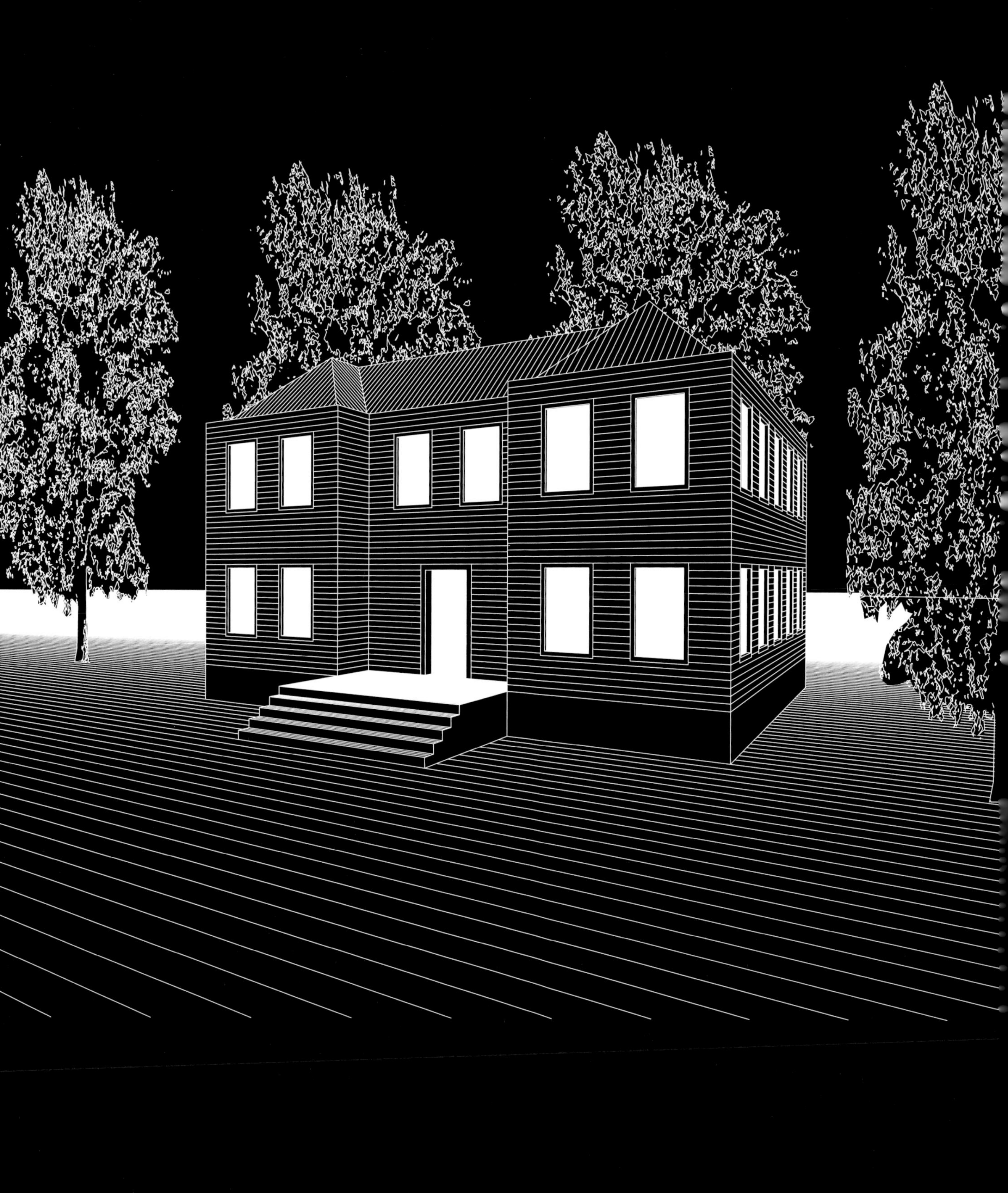

Angle
A horizontal format adjacent to a vertical block represents the classical motif of the tower villa, but here the whole does not focus on creating a picturesque appearance, as in Romantic Classicism. Life in this house is determined by two separate spheres that merge into one exciting entity – dominated by the tower.

Winkel
Ein liegendes und ein stehendes Format nebeneinander stellen das klassische Motiv der Turmvilla dar, ohne das Ganze zu einem malerischen Bild wie im romantischen Klassizismus auszumalen. Das Leben in diesem Haus wird von zwei unterschiedlichen Sphären bestimmt, die zu einem spannungsvollen Ganzen verschmelzen, das durch den Turm dominiert wird.

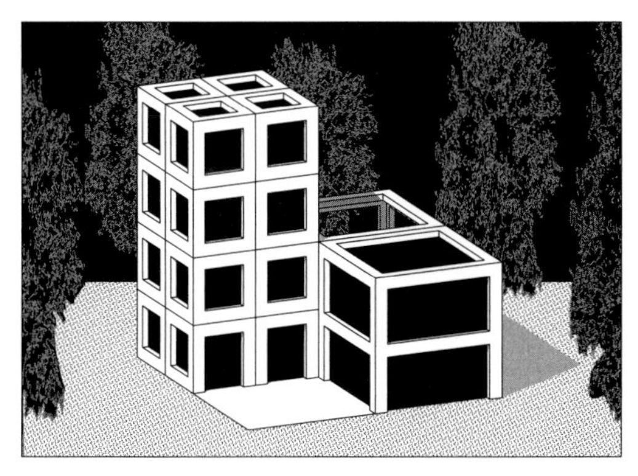 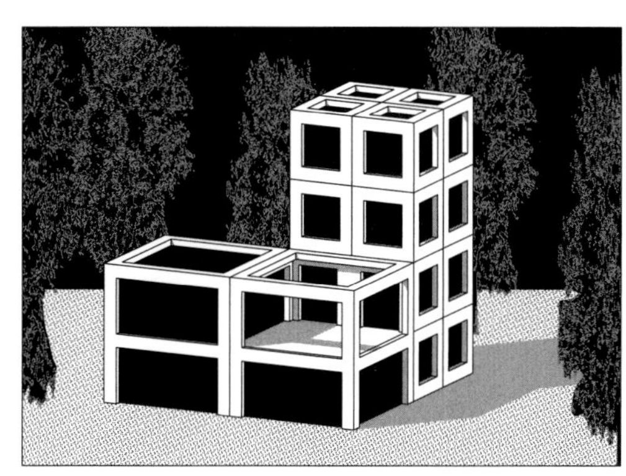

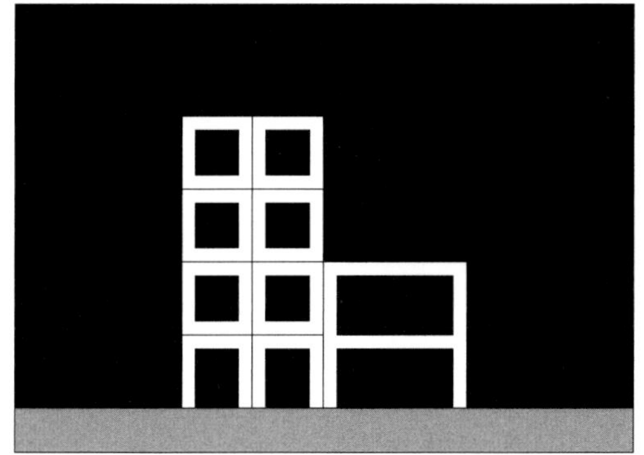 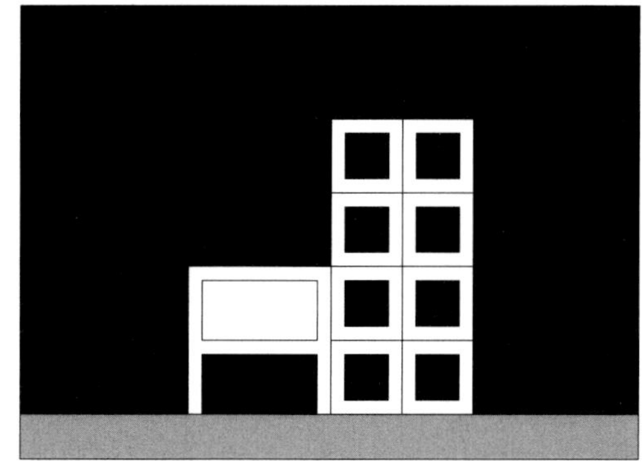

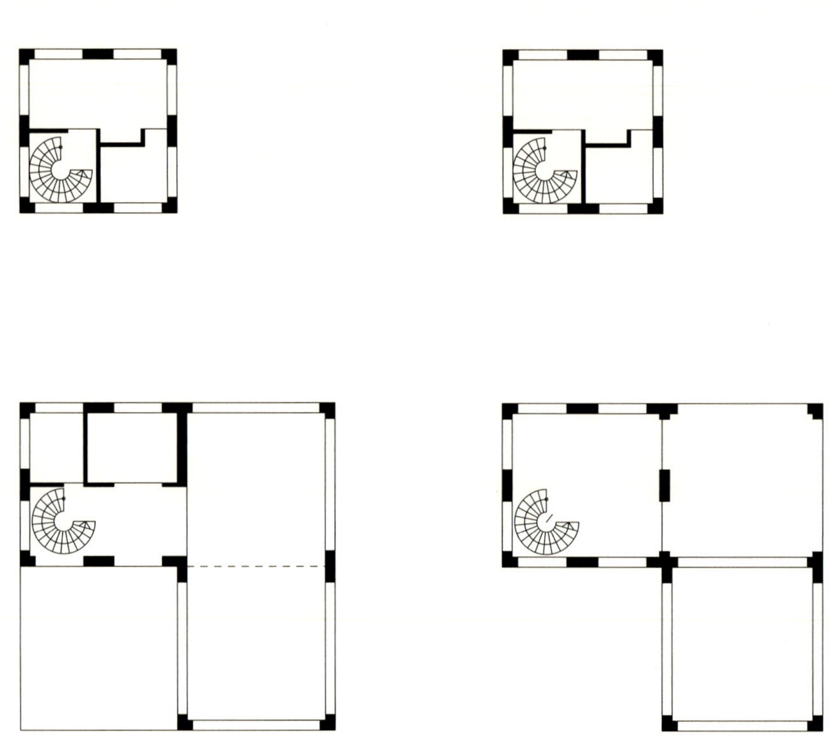

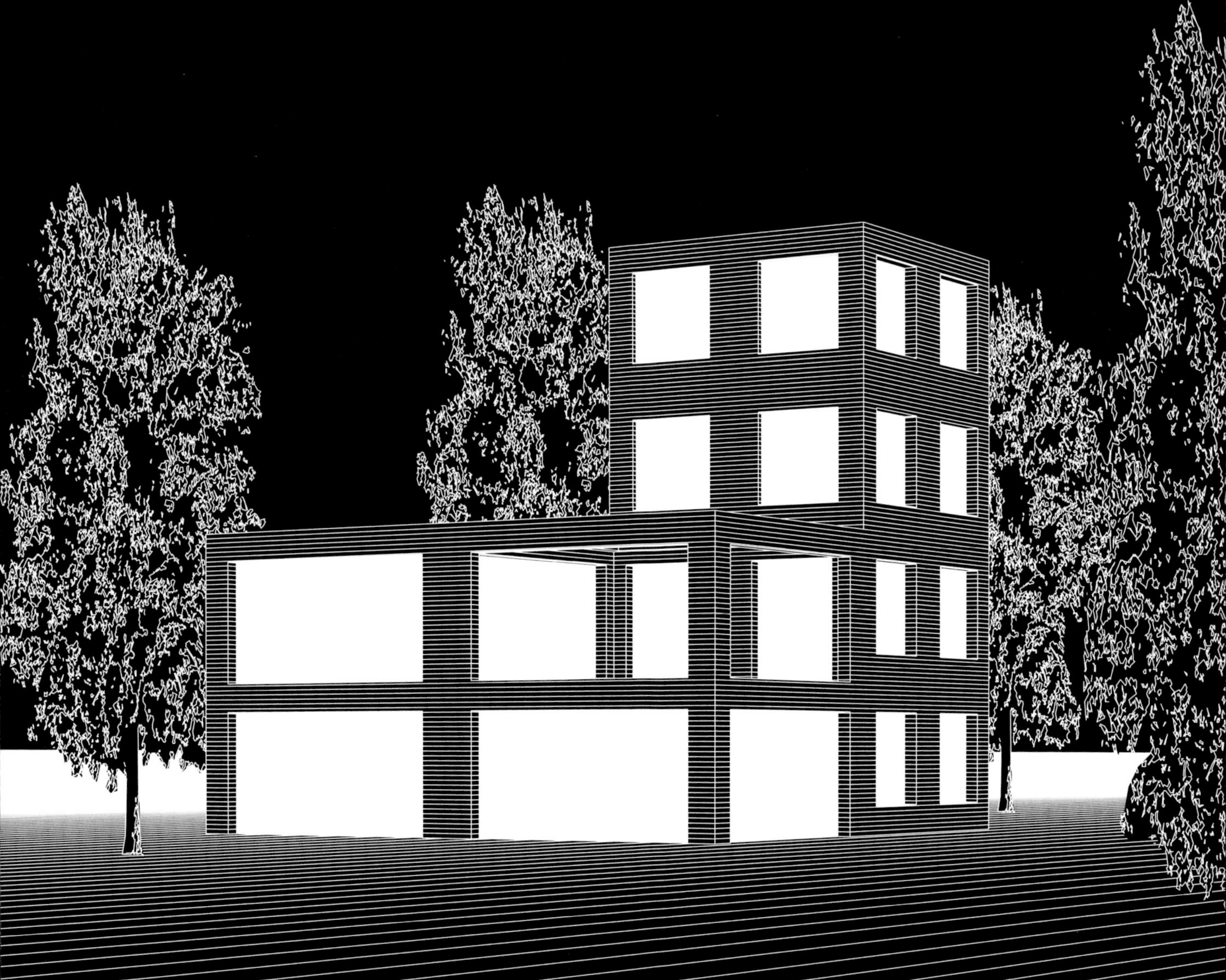

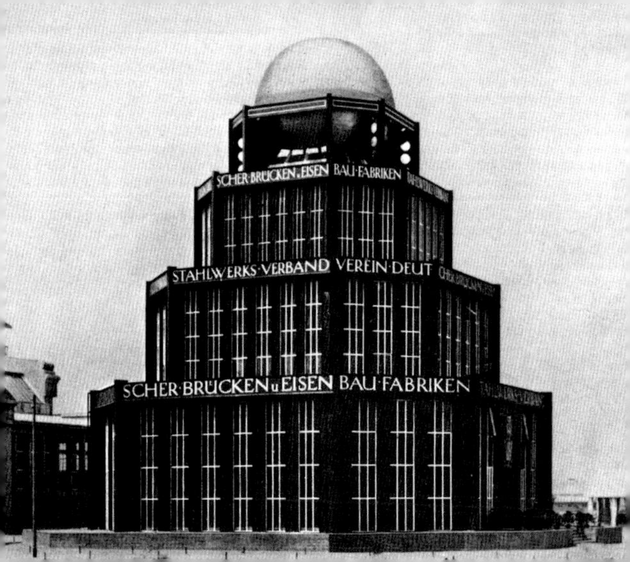
SCHER·BRÜCKEN·u·EISEN BAU·FABRIKEN
STAHLWERKS·VERBAND VEREIN·DEUT
SCHER·BRÜCKEN·u·EISEN BAU·FABRIKEN

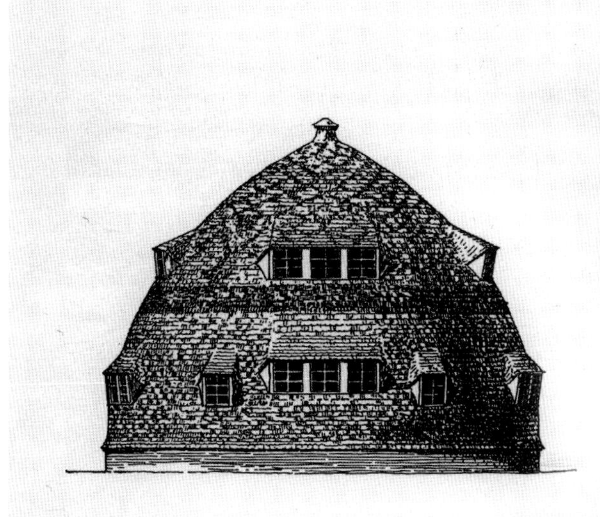

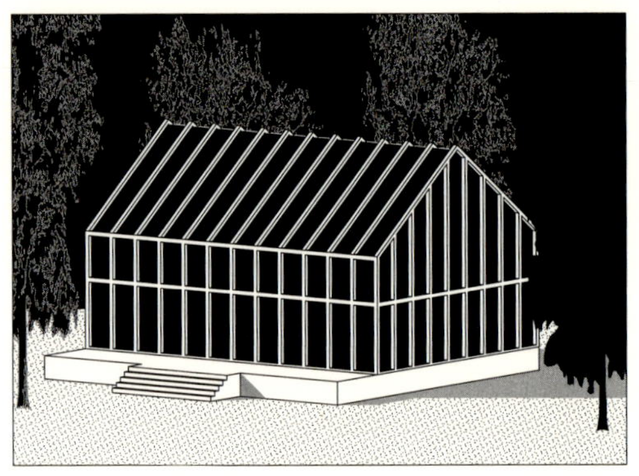 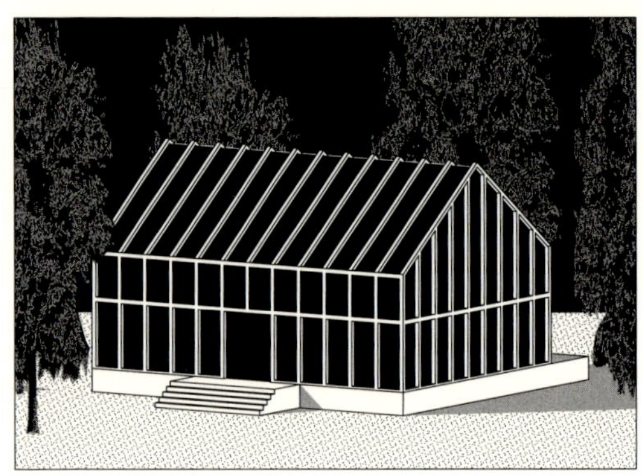

Glass House

A villa like a greenhouse. It is to be lived in as if in a botanical garden – with ample nature, inside and out. The architectonic form of the glass house is as elementary as it is attractive, characterised by the fragility with which the interior is »kept«.

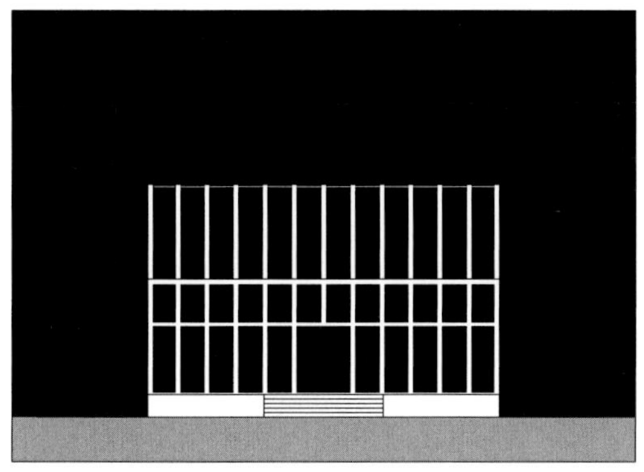 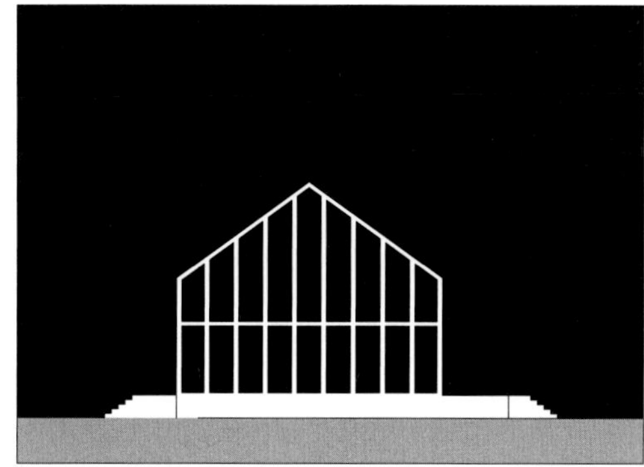

Glashaus

Eine Villa wie ein Gewächshaus. Man wohnt darin wie in einem botanischen Garten
– viel Natur, innen wie außen. Das Glashaus ist in seiner architektonischen Form
ebenso elementar wie reizvoll in seiner Zerbrechlichkeit, mit der das Innere des
Hauses »aufbewahrt« wird.

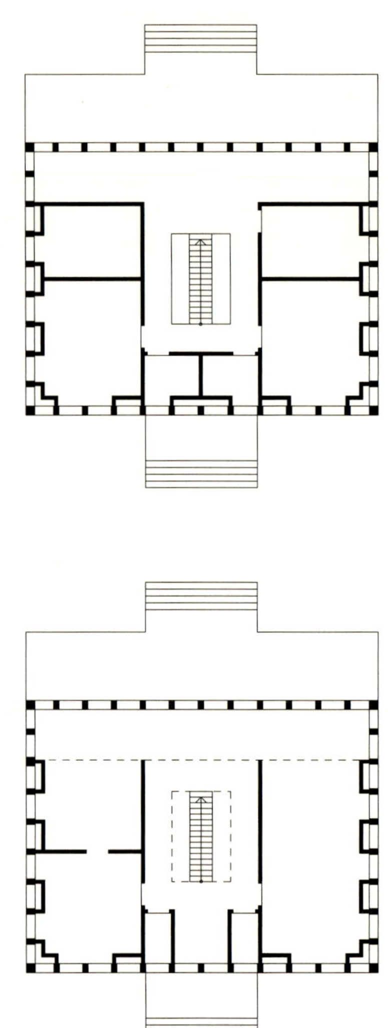

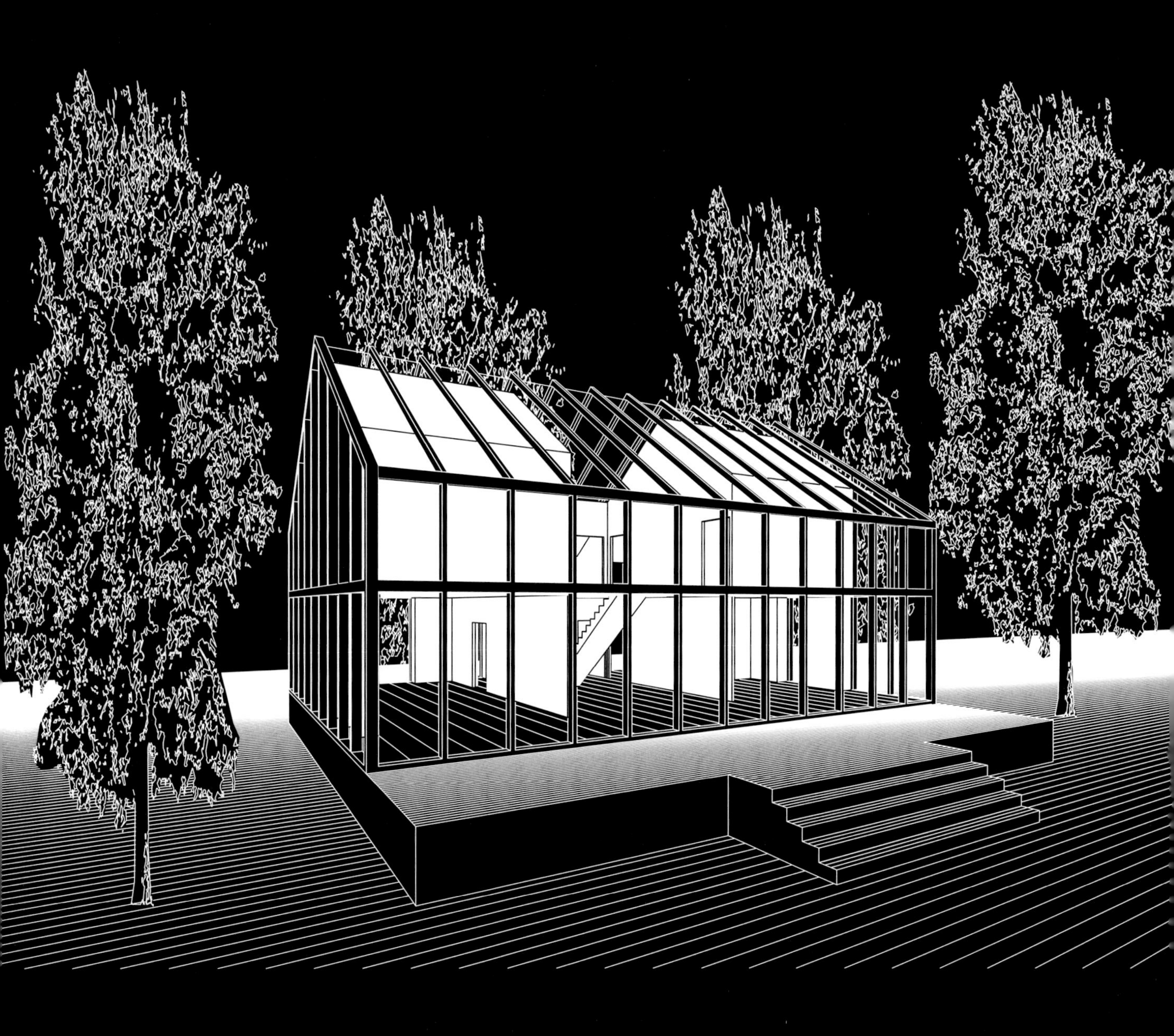

Bastion

The most important feature of the bastion is its seclusion, which also includes the large roof garden. The regular texture of the building's surface – which one could imagine, for example, built in a rough, coarse stone material – is interrupted only by an inviting doorway niche behind the entrance steps.

Bastion

Das Wichtigste an der Bastion ist ihre Abgeschlossenheit, die auch den großen Dachgarten einschließt. Die regelmäßige Textur der Oberfläche des Baukörpers, die man sich zum Beispiel in einem rauen, groben Steinmaterial gemauert vorstellen könnte, wird nur hinter der Eingangstreppe zugunsten einer einladenden Türnische unterbrochen.

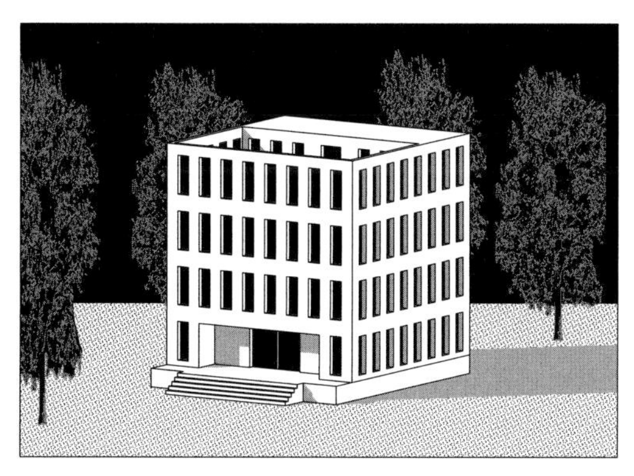
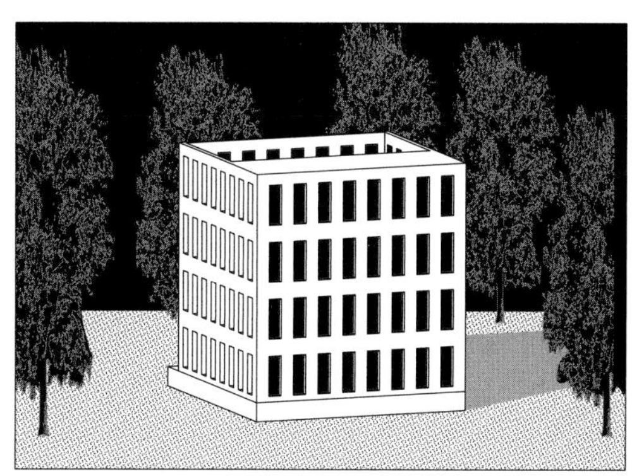
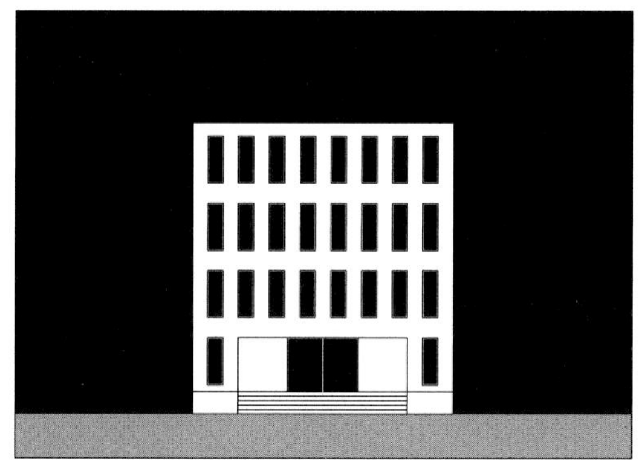
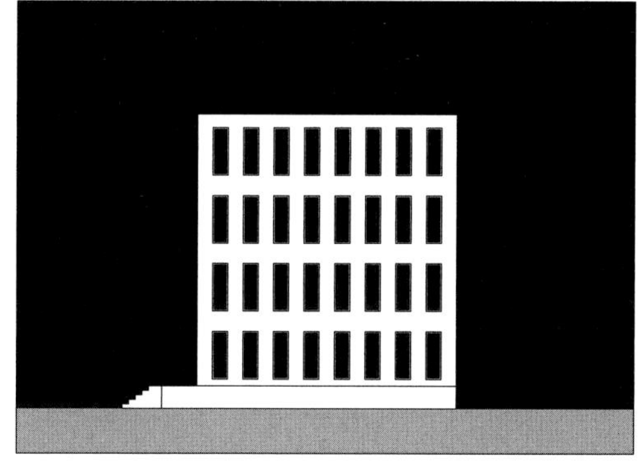

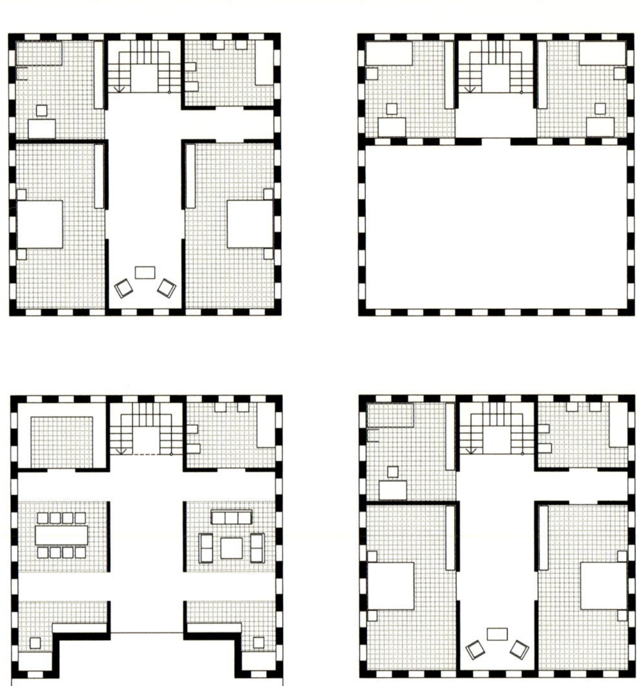

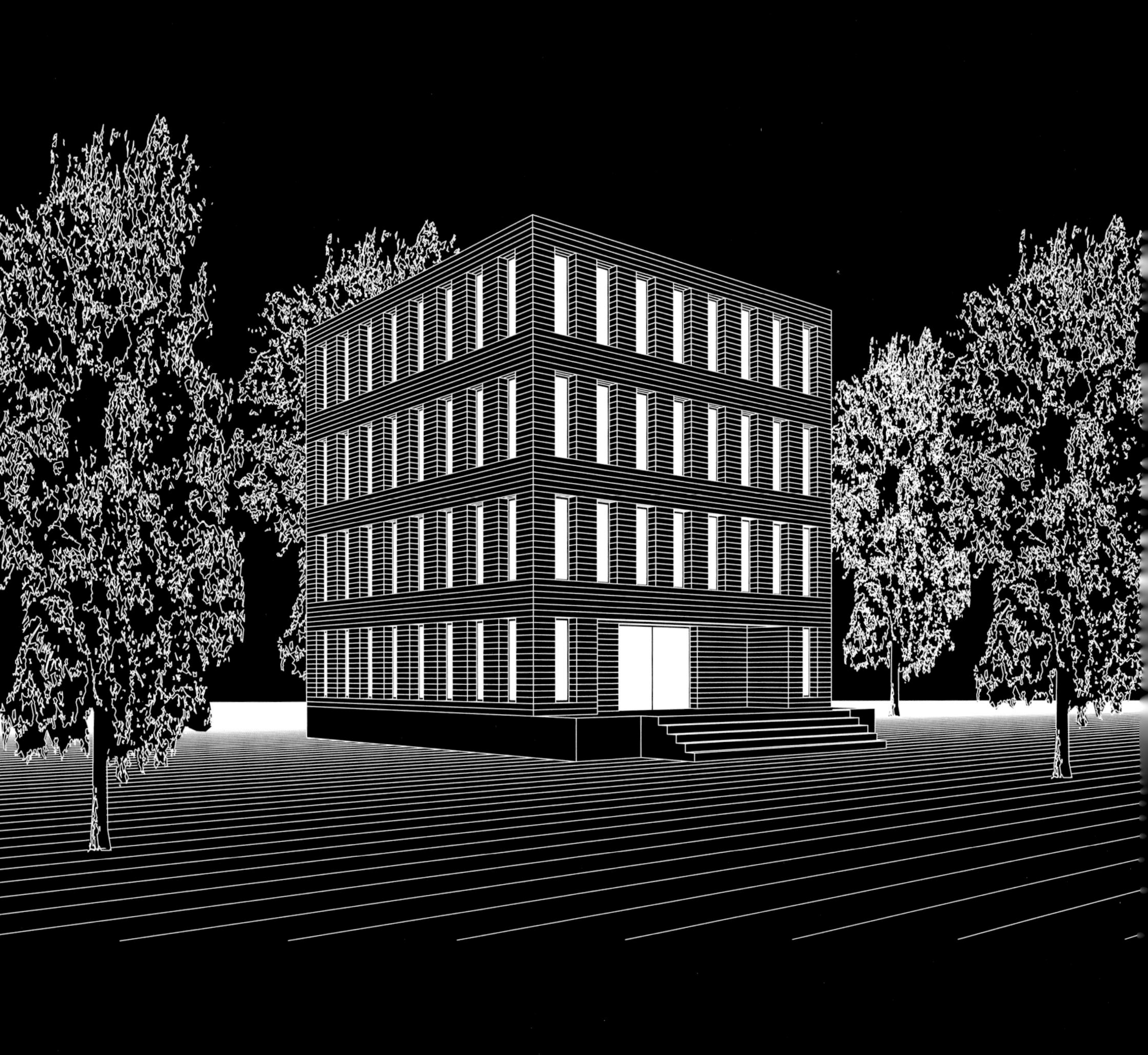

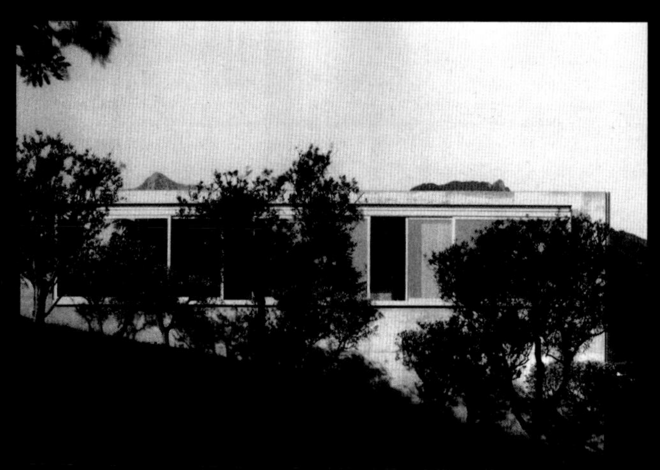

Abb. 11, 12

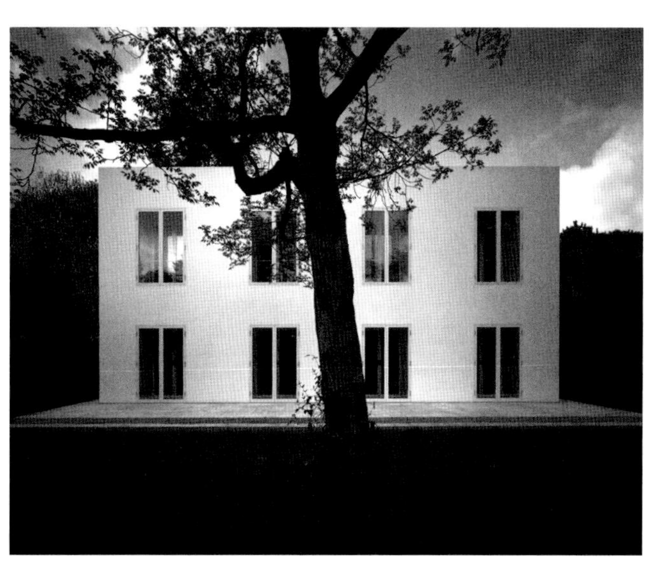

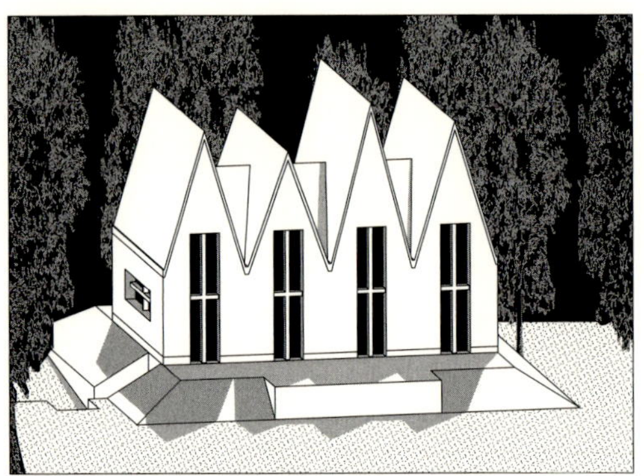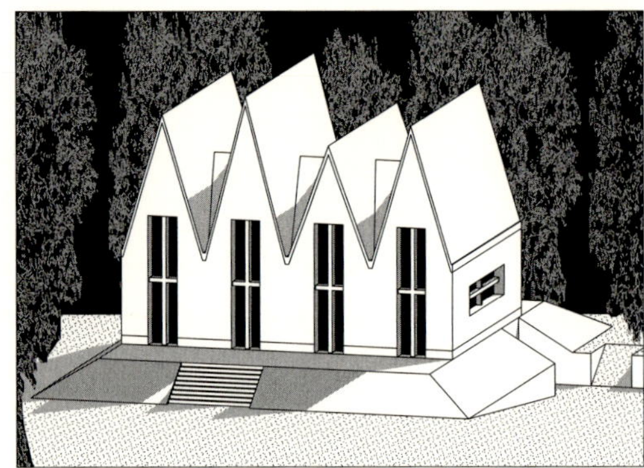

Forester's House

The silhouette of a gable between trees can only be a forester's house – as a metaphor of architecture that stands in the midst of nature, and as the pattern for a villa whose structural appearance fits harmoniously into the landscape and triggers romantic emotions.

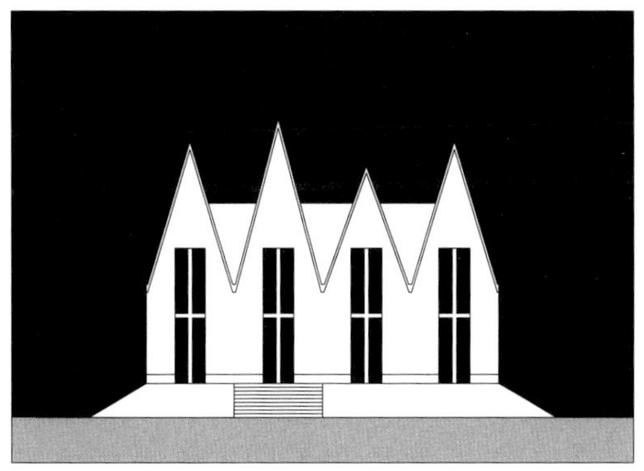 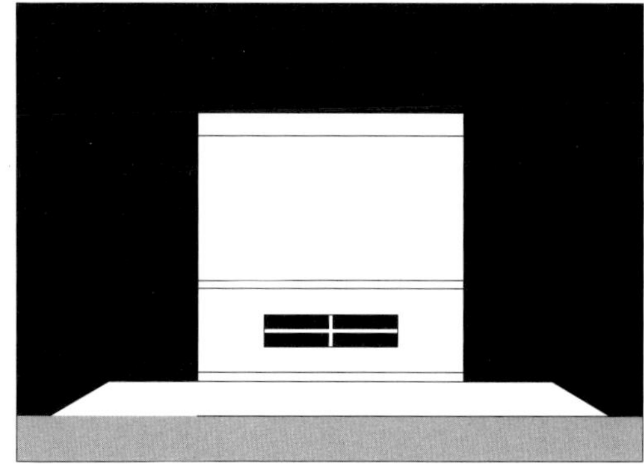

Forsthaus

Eine Giebelsilhouette zwischen Bäumen kann eigentlich nur ein Forsthaus sein – als Metapher für eine Architektur, die mitten in der Natur steht und als Vorbild für eine Villa, deren Erscheinung als Baukörper sich harmonisch in das Landschaftsbild einfügt und romantische Gefühle weckt.

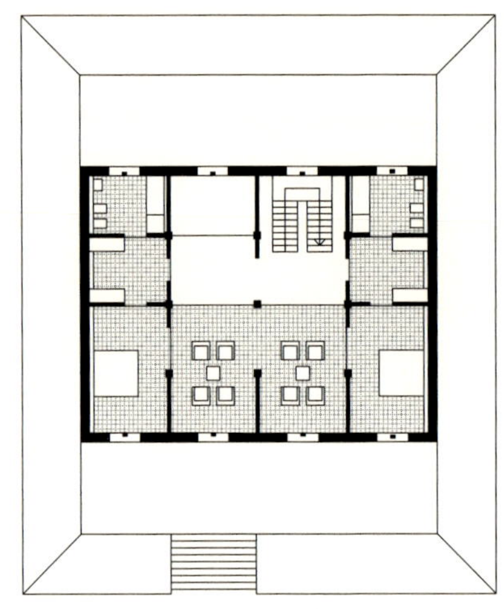

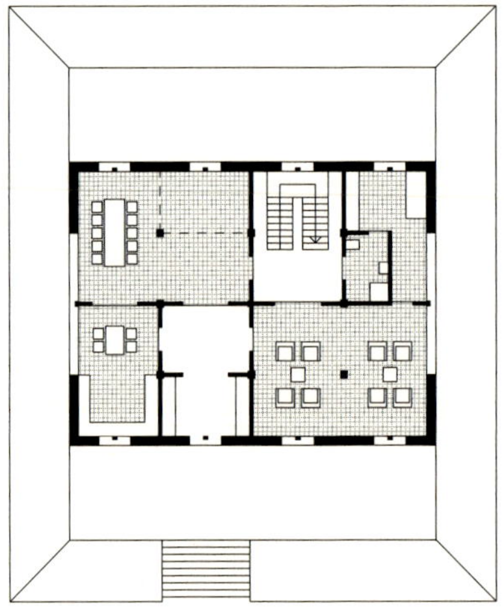

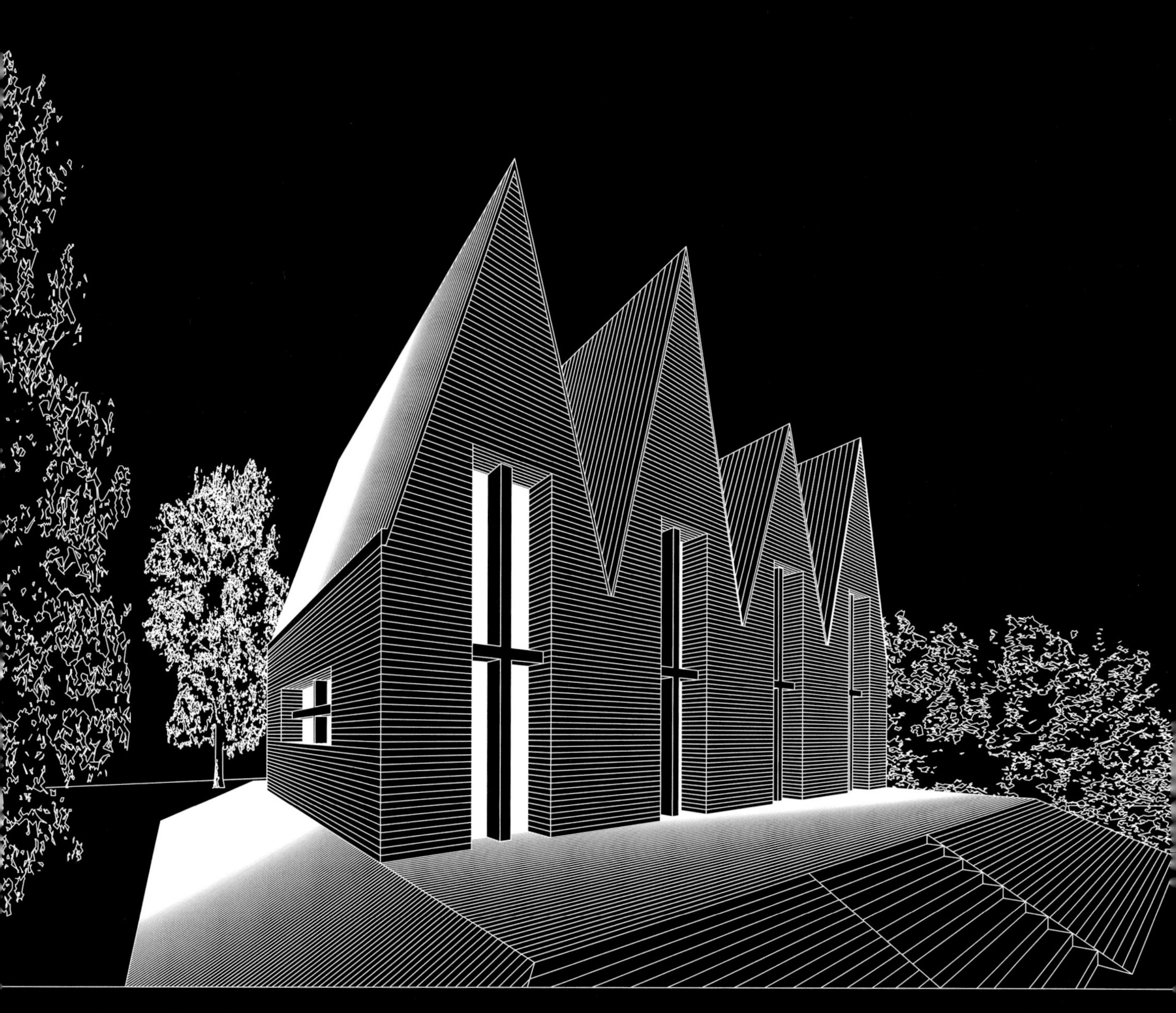

Terraced House

When its terraces are planted, like those of the Palace of Sanssouci in Potsdam, the terraced house evolves into a constructed landscape. The special atmosphere in this house is based on its extrovert character and the way that all its living spaces refer to the outside world, to nature. The one-sided orientation of these »rooms with a view« is a key feature of the terraced house.

Terrassenhaus

Das Terrassenhaus wird zur gebauten Landschaft, wenn seine Terrassen bepflanzt werden wie diejenigen des Schlosses Sanssouci in Potsdam. Die besondere Atmosphäre des Wohnens in diesem Haus beruht auf seiner Extrovertiertheit und dem Bezug aller Wohnräume zur Außenwelt, zur Natur. Die einseitige Orientierung der »Zimmer mit Aussicht« ist ein Wesensmerkmal des Terrassenhauses.

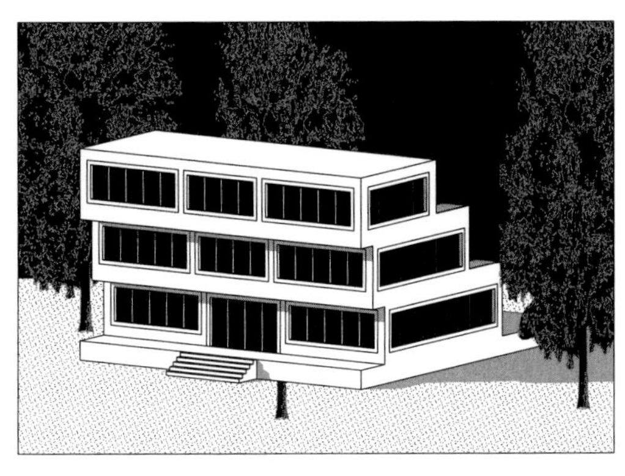
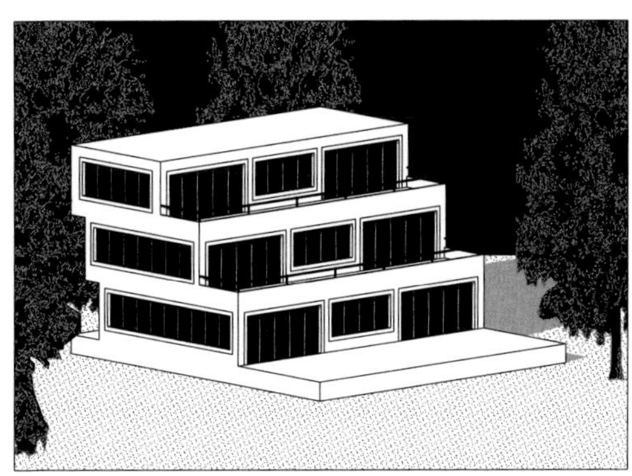
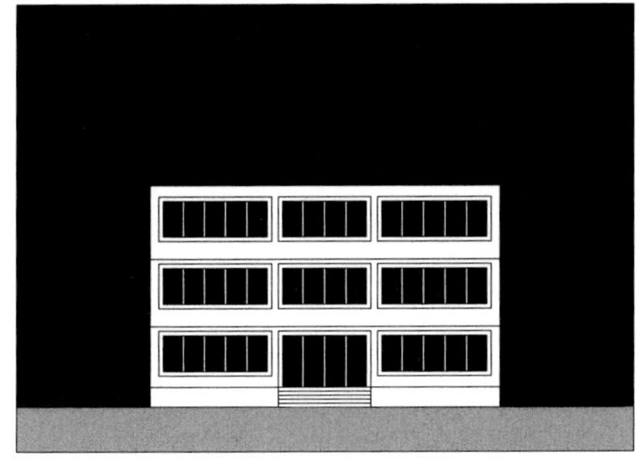
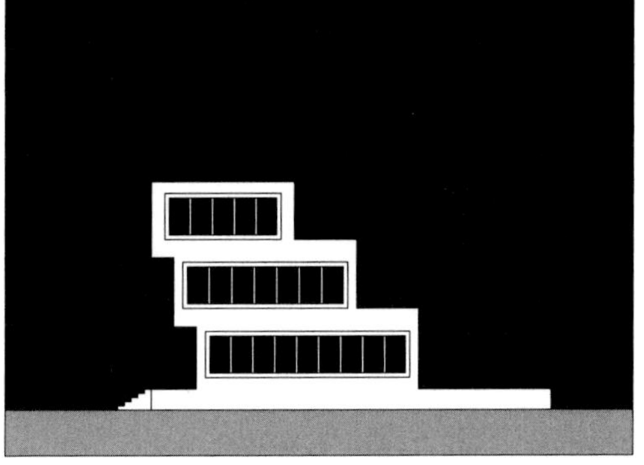

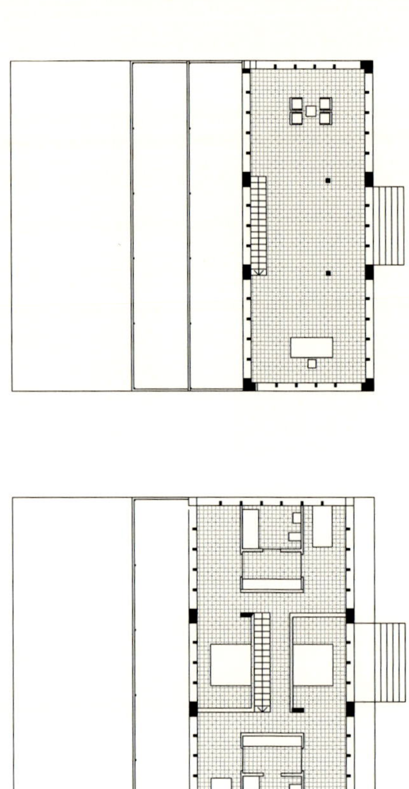
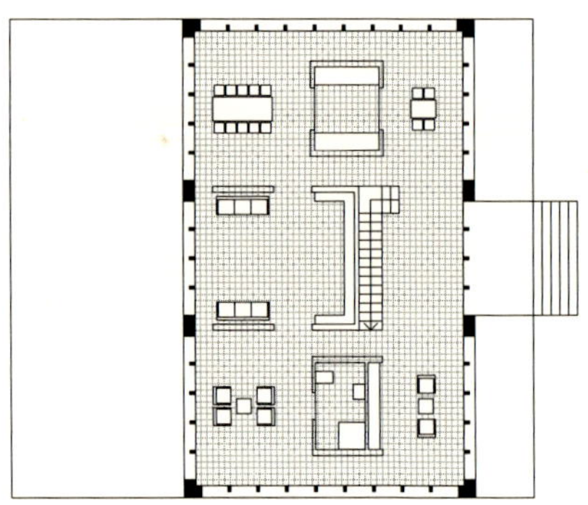

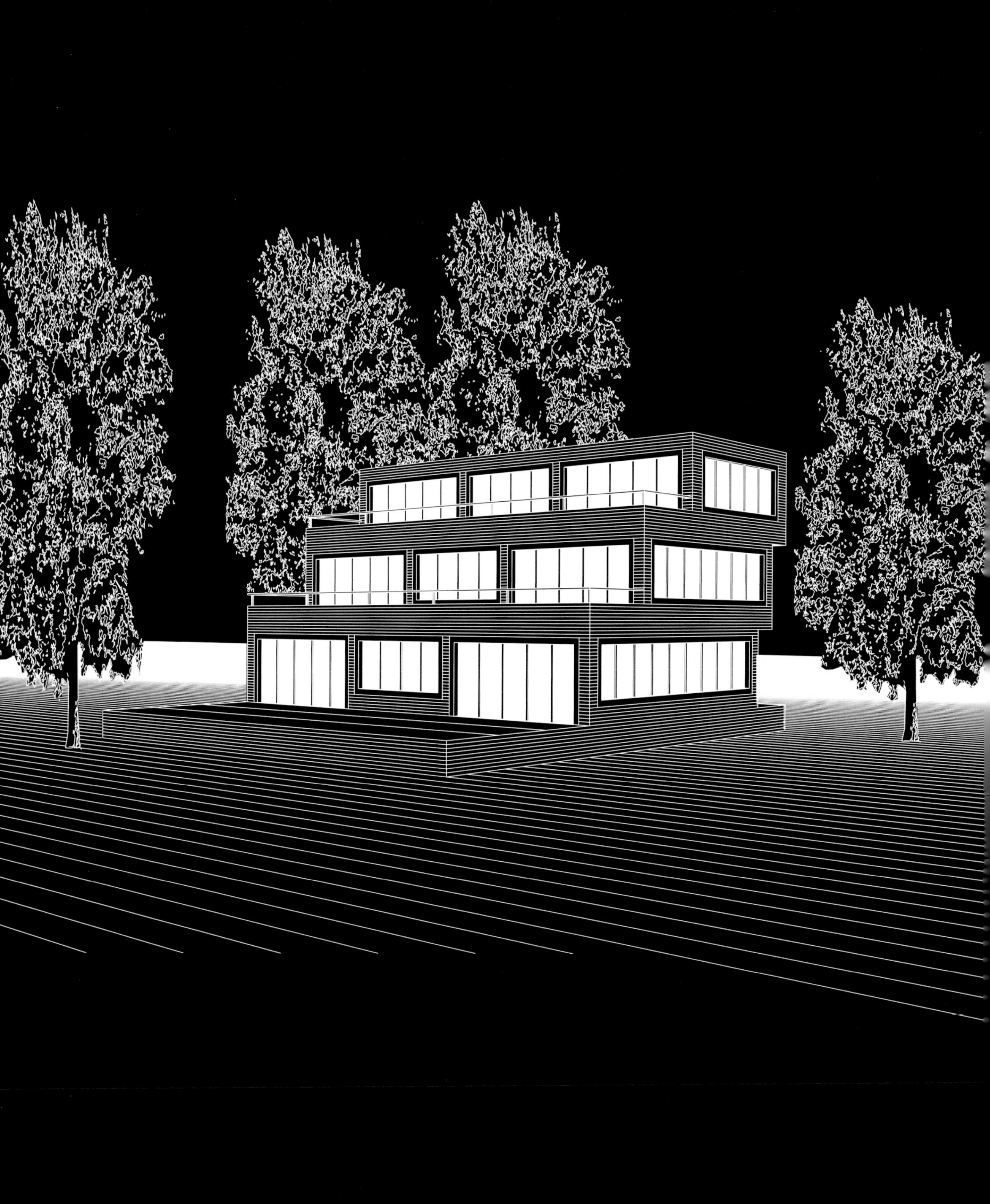

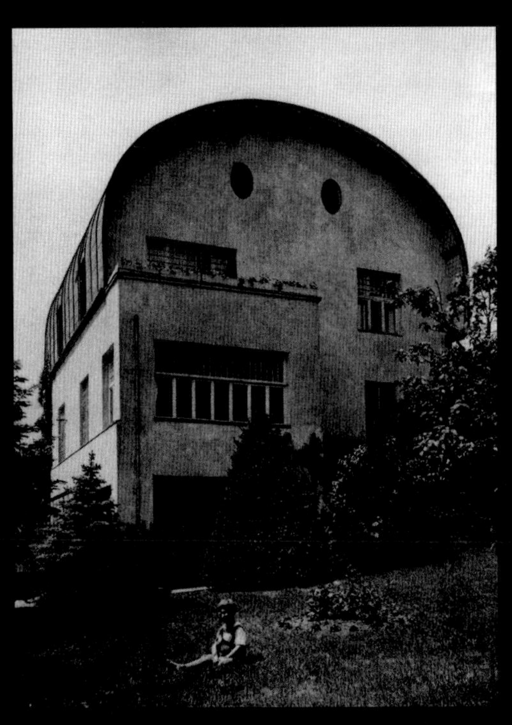

Abb. 13, 14

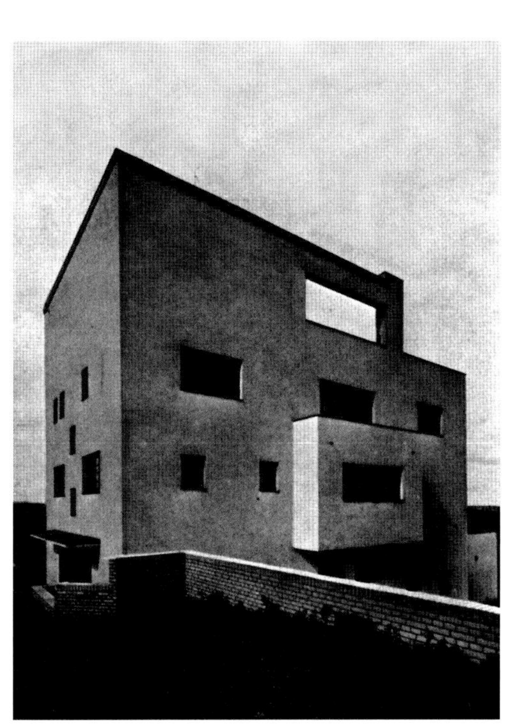

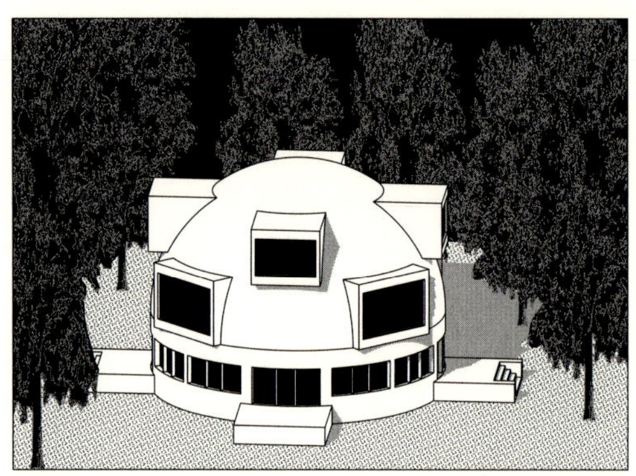 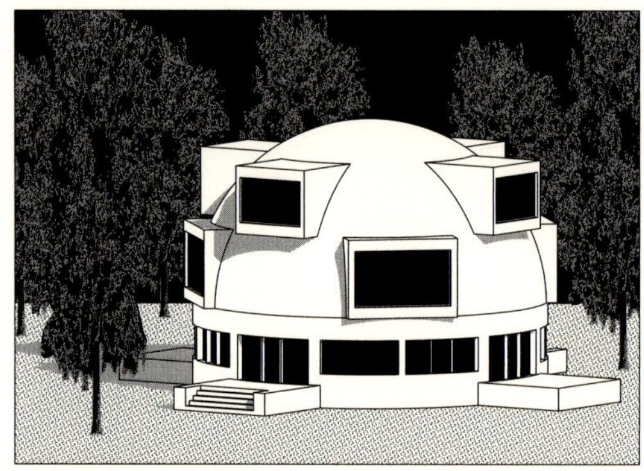

Dome

The dome creates a focus and security. It is an archetype with diverse references in architectural history, ranging across all eras and dimensions. Life in the domed house is introverted; below the roof, one feels that one is living at the centre of one's very own world – protected, as if in an igloo.

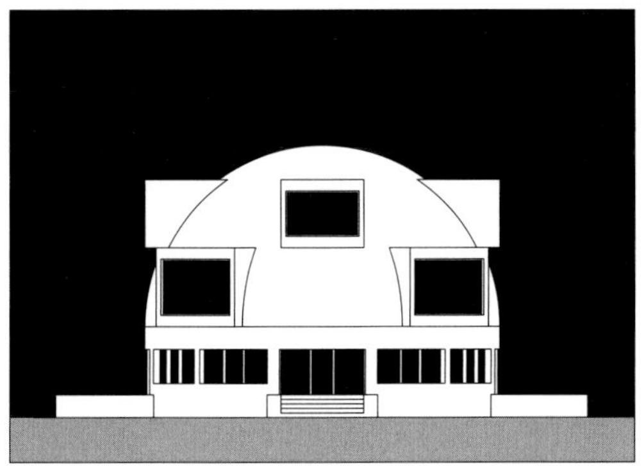 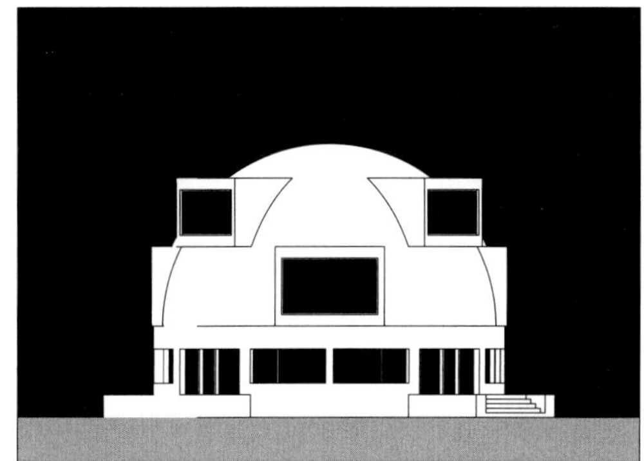

Kuppel

Die Kuppel schafft Mitte und Geborgenheit, sie ist ein Archetypus mit vielfältigen Referenzen in der Baugeschichte über alle Zeiten und Dimensionen hinweg. Im Kuppelhaus wohnt man introvertiert und unter einem Dach mit dem Gefühl, im Mittelpunkt seiner eigenen Welt zu leben – geborgen wie in einem Iglu.

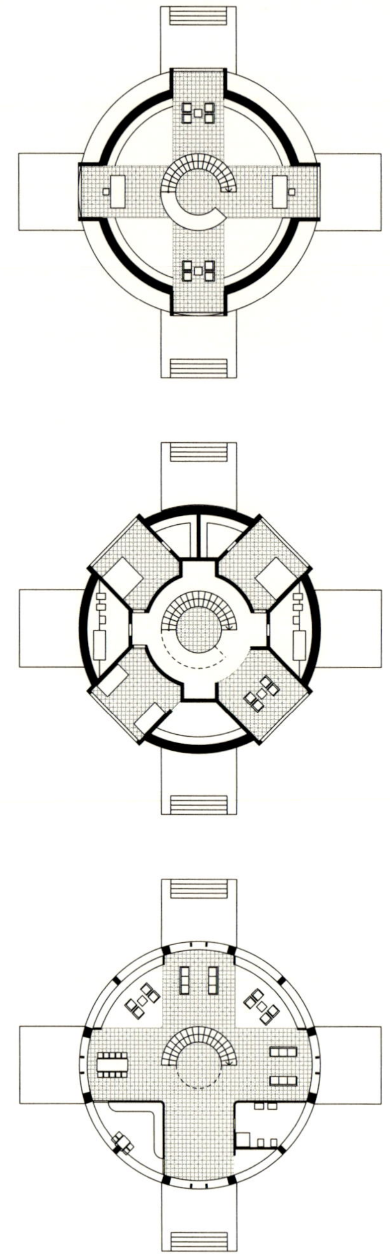

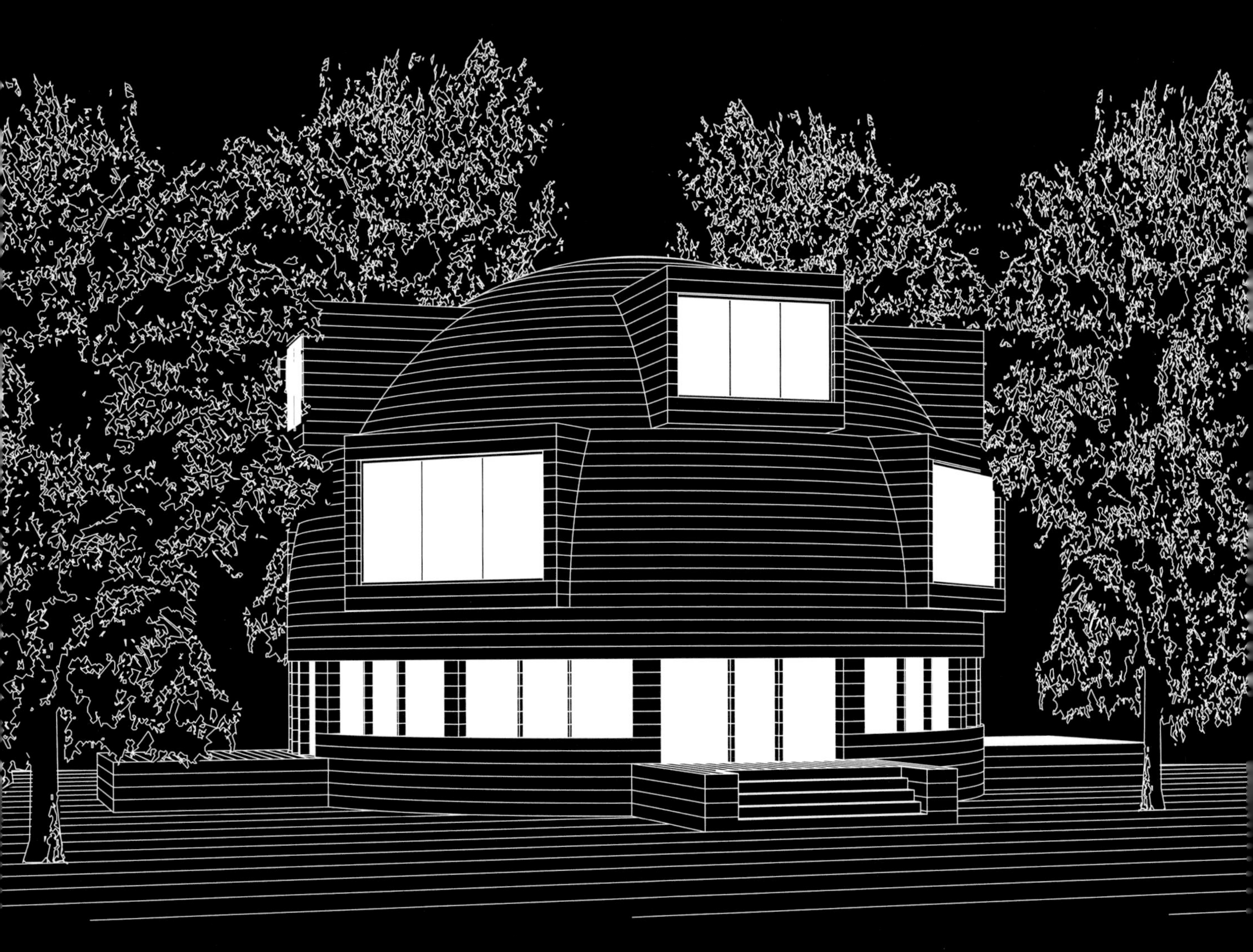

Atrium House

This house is characterised by an extreme contrast between inside and out: the free space outside and the enclosed space inside, the closed façade to the outside and the glass façade inside. Quite independent of its materialisation in a concrete project, the radical nature of this concept creates the preconditions for an individual way of life.

Atriumhaus

Es ist der extreme Gegensatz zwischen Innen und Außen, der dieses Haus auszeichnet. Der freie Raum außen und der umgrenzte innen, nach außen die geschlossene Fassade und innen die Glasfassade. Unabhängig von der Materialisierung im konkreten Projekt schafft die Radikalität der Konzeption die Voraussetzung für eine individuelle Wohnform.

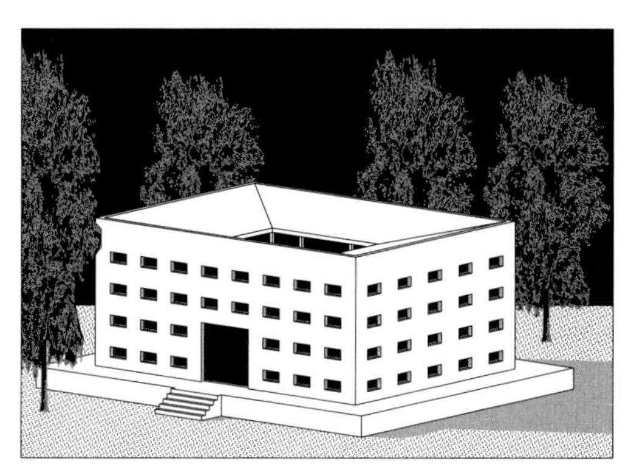
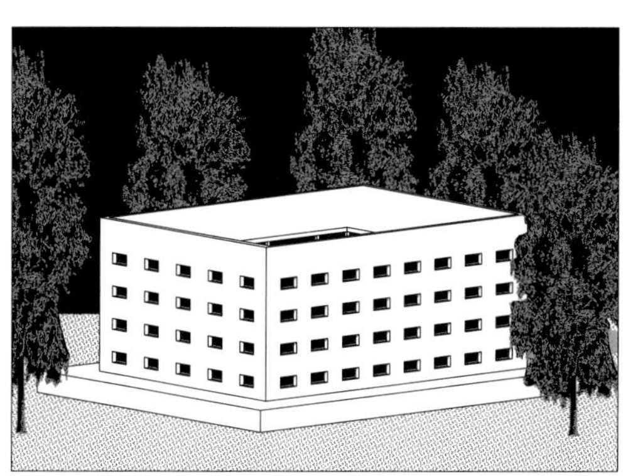
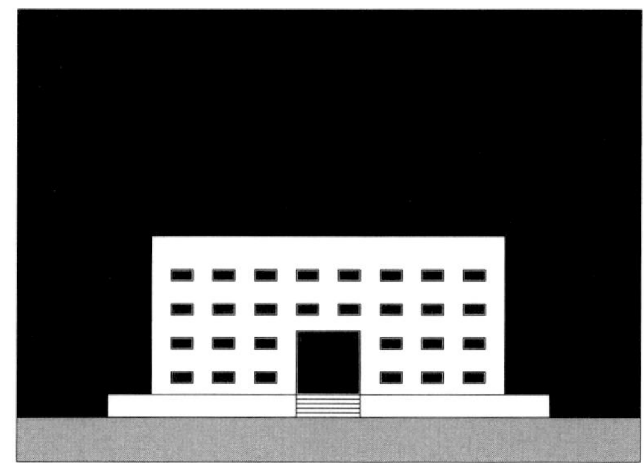
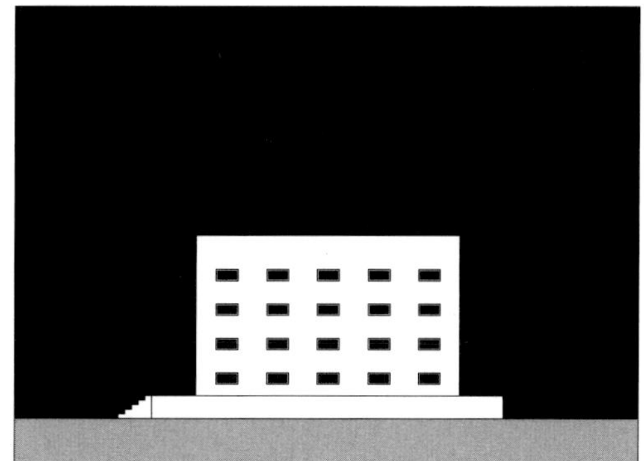

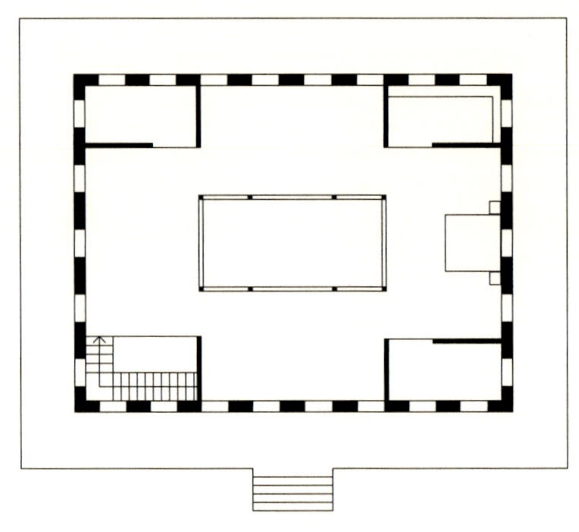

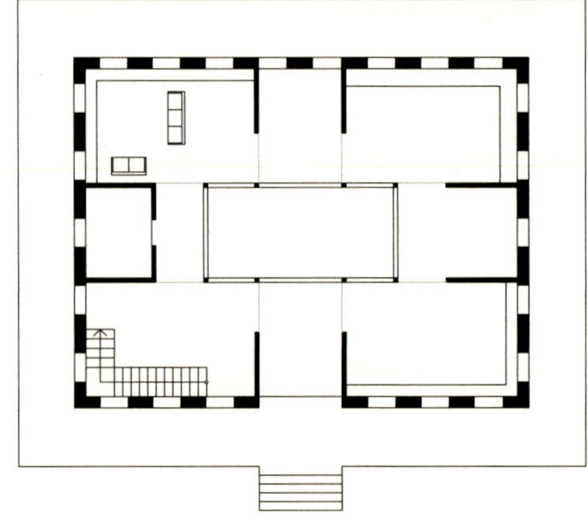

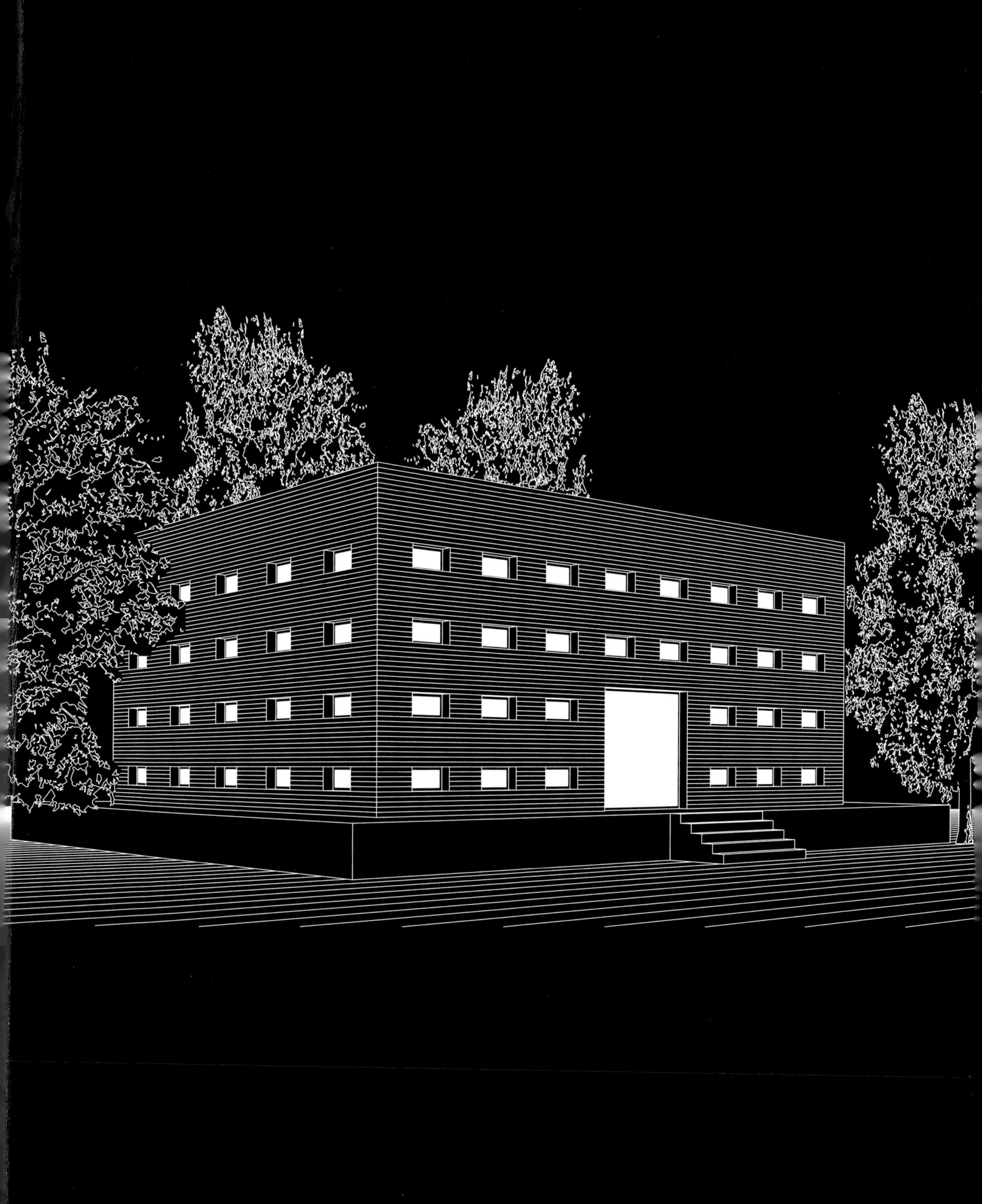

Author Autor
Klaus Theo Brenner

Collaboration Mitarbeit
Betti Plog, Jens Tränhardt

Architectonic Designs
Occasioned by an invitation to design a villa in Grunewald, Berlin, these projects were conceived together with Yakut Börekcioglu, Katrin Heßbrüggen, Britta Winkler and Orsetta Pizzoli.

Architektonische Entwürfe
Diese Entwürfe wurden zusammen mit Yakut Börekcioglu, Katrin Heßbrüggen, Britta Winkler und Orsetta Pizzoli erarbeitet. Anlass war die Aufforderung, eine Villa im Grunewald in Berlin zu entwerfen.

Pictures Abbildungen
1, 2 Claude-Nicolas Ledoux, Maison de Campagne, aus: *Architecture de Ledoux, Inédits pour un Tome III*, Paris 1991
3 Andrea Palladio, Villa Rotonda, aus: s. unten · 4 Le Corbusier, Villa Savoie aus: Colin Rowe, *Die Mathematik der idealen Villa*, Basel 1998 · 5, 6 Erwin Heerich, Museumsinsel Hombroich · 7 A. Libera und C. Malaparte: Casa Malaparte, Capri aus: *Freiräume, Häuser die Geschichte machten*, München 1998 · 8 Mies van der Rohe, Farnsworth House aus: Werner Blaser, *Mies van der Rohe, Farnsworth House*, Basel 1999 · 9 Bruno Taut, Monument des Eisens
10 Bruno Taut, Parkwächterhaus · 11 Livio Vacchini, Haus Vacchini, aus: Werner Blaser, *Transformation*, Basel 1994
12 Oswald Matthias Ungers, Haus Ungers, Foto: Stefan Müller · 13 Adolf Loos, Haus Horner, aus: s. unten
14 Adolf Loos, Villa Müller aus: Adolf Loos, *Villen*, Wien 2001 · Alle anderen Abbildungen: Klaus Theo Brenner

Translation Übersetzung: Lucinda Rennison, Berlin
Design and setting Gestaltung und Satz: Dirk Biermann, Potsdam
Printing and binding Druck und Bindung: OAN Offizin Andersen Nexö, Leipzig, Zwenkau

Bibliographic information published by Die Deutsche Bibliothek
Die Deutsche Bibliothek lists this publication in the Deutsche Nationalbibliographie;
detailed bibliographic data are available in the Internet at http://dnb.ddb.de
Bibliographische Information Der Deutschen Bibliothek
Die Deutsche Bibliothek verzeichnet diese Publikation in der Deutschen Nationalbibliographie;
detaillierte bibliographische Daten sind im Internet über http://dnb.ddb.de abrufbar.

jovis Verlag
Kurfürstenstraße 15/16
10785 Berlin

www.jovis.de

ISBN 3-936314-70-5